A HUNGARIAN QUARTET

Four Contemporary Short Novels

A HUNGARIAN QUARTET

Four Contemporary Short Novels

Géza Ottlik
LOGBOOK

Iván Mándy
LEFT BEHIND

Miklós Mészöly
FORGIVENESS

Péter Esterházy
THE TRANSPORTERS

CORVINA

Published by Corvina Books, Budapest
Vörösmarty tér 1. Hungary 1051

Selection by Mária Kőrösy

ISBN 963 13 3366 3
Printed in Hungary 1991
Szeged Printing House, Szeged

CONTENTS

GÉZA OTTLIK

LOGBOOK

Translated by John Bátki

A Danish story for Iván

Captain Kirketerp, while being a chauvinist, was not a patriot. With remarkable self-restraint he was going over the odds for the third time. He had to make a sober estimate of the prospects, all the while knowing perfectly well that he was irrationally pulling for a compatriot's victory. Only a moment ago he caught himself weighing the chances of this gal Astrid actually reaching the finals. Well, he'd better forget about that at once. Let's just say that with the luck of the draw she could get past her preliminary heat.

Captain Kirketerp himself had been a hurdler once, sixty years ago. For a while he and his best friend Skjoldborg had taken turns holding the junior record. But Harestrup had been faster. He was no longer alive. Neither was Jens nor Sophus Moeller whose Danish record had been exactly what this Astrid Andersen ran last year to receive a pretty decent world ranking. Given a good start, she just might qualify from her heat.

All right, all right, Captain Kirketerp thought, take it easy. No longer was he a hurdler and he was barely a Captain, without a ship for twenty years. Denmark had no ports left, no seaboard, ever since the Swedes, those treacherous allies, having chased out the Visigoths and the English, proceeded to take over the country only to be expelled by the Russians who were in turn ousted by the Marquesas warriors who gave away even more Danish territory to the neighbors. Gone was Schleswig-Holstein; their ancient province Norway had been lost in the time of the Swedes, and after the Polynesian takeover Aarhus and the heart of Jutland was practically all that was left. And the conquerors had been progressively worse, according to Kirketerp. The English protectorate had been preferable to the Swedes, while under the Czars, although converted to Greek Orthodoxy, they kept their Christianity as well as the Danish monarchy (albeit under another name and transformed into an absolute autocracy) — whereas the current Marquesan dominion outlawed all religions and abolished

9

the monarchy. The country became a tribal sub-chieftainship and received a new name. No one, except for athletes, was allowed across the lines of demarcation. They, as for example this Astrid Andersen now in Paris, could still use, as a matter of fact it was compulsory for them to use, the designation Denmark (in parentheses) in order to demonstrate that theirs was a free and independent nation, which was not the case. And so the Captain was a chauvinist but at the same time not a patriot.

Astrid easily made it past the first two heats, both times bettering her personal best. Captain Kirketerp, again relying on superlative self-restraint, refused to speculate on her further chances. What about the semifinals? What will be, will be. We have already done well, he reflected. Astrid came in a strong second in both heats. But when—after an explosive start—she outright won her semifinal heat, reaching the finals with the best time in the entire field, it was all over for the Captain's otherwise rock-steady self-control. Astrid, surrounded by sportswriters and TV-reporters, commented ecstatically, "Wow! So far, so good." You bet, thought the Captain. Wow indeed! A Viking in the finals! Sports history was in the making, for this was the first World Championship of its kind, to be held henceforth every two years. The top three finishers were certain to be noted, and if Astrid were to get off the blocks that well in the finals ... who knows, a Danish bronze might enter the books ... (and of course, what counted most for him, his own Logbook in the morning) ... But could that ever happen, even with a new Danish record, that third place? Get serious, Harald, the Captain chided himself.

Ah, if Sophus were here, and Skjoldborg, the old boys ... the "palisaders" ... They would have more information on Astrid's world-class opponents in the finals ... But wait! There was his faithful friend Ivo Maandygaard! Ivo knew everything. So one half hour before Astrid's showdown he scurried over to Admiral Maandygaard's place on Aulichgade.

"If all goes well," said the Admiral, "Miss Andersen might squeeze into fifth, possibly fourth place." 'But for that to happen, she should not get off the blocks quite so spectacularly,' he thought, 'it was a mistake to do that in the semifinals.'

'But it worked!' the Captain thought, bewildered.

'That was an accident. Sheer luck.'

'And—talent.'

'Native talent? Even more of an accident, blind luck. Believe me, Harald. You'll see, just watch her in the finals.'

Kirketerp believed him. Maandygaard already at the age of twenty-six had made Vice Admiral, while the highest he ever got to be was Captain. That was the way things were; and twenty years ago his squadron had been taken away just the same as Maandygaard's entire fleet. All in all, thought the Captain, they had weathered these landlocked twenty years quite well.

"Like hell we did, Commodore," said Maandygaard angrily, and shot a glance behind his back. Obviously he was able to read Kirketerp's unspoken thoughts in the depths of the Captain's eyes. Also, he promoted him.

"You are always right, Ivo," said the Commodore, automatically casting a glance behind his back. The use of the formal mode of address was strictly forbidden, and even tête-à-tête they were supposed to address each other as *Tai.* This was rebellion on their part, open mutiny which any witness would immediately have to report for fear of himself becoming a traitor to the nation—or rather, to the sub-chieftainship. But there was no one else in the room.

"Well, to tell the truth, I haven't weathered it well either," said Kirketerp. "Quite lousily, in fact. I still have to grit my teeth each time I do the compulsory—although beautiful and charming—ritual dances. It's too much. Worse yet is that Taboo—or *Tepu,* that is, the Sacred and Forbidden. The constant celebration of totem animals, those 'sacrifices' for them. All the old meanings of the Danish language are Taboo, the library is Taboo, that we could live with, but sailing is Taboo, and sailing is a must, and walking on two feet is Taboo, a hardship especially on our youth; I tell you Ivo, this will lead to trouble."

"Look, Harald, these people have been living in peace and harmony on their Marquesas Islands, tall and stately, exceptionally courageous and intelligent, their civilization ancient and highly developed—why, even their navigational expertise stumps us, the way they crisscrossed, conquered and colonized the endless reaches of the Pacific Ocean in their outrigger canoes; but

11

what is truly incomprehensible for our puffed-up European arrogance is why they abandoned their conquests and wanderings about seven or eight hundred years ago. The fact is they had been prospering without a care on their lush island paradises when we erupted upon them with our civilization and Christianity, bringing misery, contagious diseases and an unprecedented rapid deterioration. So now the pathetic remnants of their tribe, mortally reduced in numbers, body and soul, have finally found themselves the weaponry with which to set out on their wanderings and conquests again."

All this was no news to Kirketerp. The Admiral, who was not known to make long speeches, could have merely said, "Schundtvig," but now with the pole-vault dragging out interminably on the screen he became concerned that the anxious anticipation of Astrid's finals would make his friend ill with excitement, so he wanted to snap the Captain out of his temporary attack of chauvinism by restoring his usual unpatriotism. First he tried an old Charleston:

"Yes, sir, that's my baby…" but Kirketerp ignored him. Next, he attempted: "I want to be happy…" But this was dismissed by a wave of the hand. Now the history of the Marquesas Islands could always be relied on to claim Harald's undivided attention, and this time was no different. So that by the time the pole vault was mercifully over the Commodore was deeply involved with the topic. He turned off the television.

'Schundtvig,' he thought. 'And anchor chain, goatsnudge. I can see what is on Ivo's mind.'

They had been cadets together at the Royal Danish Naval Academy where their instructor happened to be Schundtvig, the most ferocious maniac at the school. Petty Officer Schundtvig crushed their self-esteem, rubbed out every trace of their human dignity. One evening before taps Kirketerp, driven to the usual daily despair by the usual daily round of outrageous humiliations, was examining the cable of the smaller anchor in the stern, trying to see if it could be untied. He succeeded; he lifted the thing, then tied it back. He did not notice one of his classmates appearing behind his back, watching what he was doing. It was Ivo Maandygaard.

By then Kirketerp knew the names of the others. The only other thing he knew was that none of them felt the way he did. Many had cried night and day, even in their sleep, but when—to console or to seek sympathy—he would offer some comment on Schundtvig ("He's an animal"), they merely turned their backs on him.

As did Maandygaard, once. A shrug was his only response. Now, however, in the twilight on the stern, stepping behind cadet Kirketerp he delivered a "goatsnudge". He gently bumped the other's backside with his knee. The way one's older brother would have. Kirketerp spun around in a huff and they eyed each other without a word.

Ever since then they have been able to read each other's unspoken thoughts.

This had been very important back then because, were they to use Danish words, entire novels, volumes and volumes could not have spoken what Maandygaard had to say. "Schundtvig? Ah yes. We have him, all right." "Anchor chain? Yes, it can be untied. So you too have found out about that, Kirketerp. Around your neck and into the water with you and the anchor. Good to know that. Useful." "This is what we've got. Nothing else. Only this." "You will put up with it, Harald. You will survive." "But we need time." "In the end we shall benefit enormously from this. That means you too, Harald." (Plus a few volumes' worth of Danish words which would come to them later, forty and sixty years later.)

'My God,' thought Commodore Kirketerp, 'it has been more than sixty years since that wordless "goatsnudge" and to this day what strength it gives, how clear its meaning. Tell me, Ivo, isn't it the Maoris who possess such mysteriously charged words? Such as your fraternal kick in the ass?'

"Quite possibly," said Maandygaard. "We'll get back to this, but right now I think it is getting to be time for the finals. Miss Andersen's finals. We might as well call her *Tai, Tai* Astrid, with a clear conscience, if you know what I mean?"

"I get it. They, the pathetic remnants of the once highly civilized islanders whom we have devastated, have come back to triumph over us at last—using our own barbaric methods—and

13

instead of exterminating us, they are trying to help and improve us, so why insult them by refusing to use their important words. (Well then I too would rather say *Tai* in place of one of our Danish translations such as 'Sister Astrid' or 'soul mate' or 'sister-in-arms'...)"

"Turn on that old Mihalyson television, Rear Admiral," said Ivo. Unlike his friend, he was neither a chauvinist, nor unpatriotic, but this did not change the fact of their thinking and feeling in exactly the same way. "You know I still use that old Mihalyson..."

"I know," said Kirketerp. "Same as ever. But if you insist on promoting me every five minutes, I am going to be your superior officer in ten minutes, and will read you one of my poems, so help me." He clicked on the set to the coverage of the Paris event.

Packed stadium, standing room only, flags, ministers in the special box seats; the camera zooms in on the field, the faces at the competitors' entrance, more shots of the French champion, naturally, than of Astrid. Tension and excitement in the air. Another shot of Astrid. After she had qualified for the finals with the best time, reporters surrounded her, asking for some comment. He had to tell Ivo. "Do you know what she said, grinning insanely?"

"What?"

"Wow, so far, so good."

Yes, the Admiral, too, likes that, well enough to file it away. Wow, so far, so good.

"And what about the finals?" Astrid had shrugged. "Anything may happen there..."

Well naturally. Even if she finishes last (according to form), even then she will have brought the Danish colors to world prominence. Now even the Admiral begins to give some thought to how many, and which ones, among her great opponents could she beat for the bronze medal that would make (sports) history. For when it is announced that she has been assigned the center track next to the French girl, he nods at Kirketerp. "That's good!" Better still, she is flanked by another great runner on the other side. These two should pull *Tai* Astrid along. "If only she'd get off to a more relaxed start..."

The whole stadium is one enormous uproar, even the bleachers have caught the fever. Then a profound silence settles in. The first start is called back. Ow. Was that Astrid? She too had jumped the gun... No! It is the French girl who receives the warning red flag. Good, maybe now she will have to play it safe with a less fiery start. Ow. Like hell she is playing it safe. Off with the gun, she is a meter ahead of Astrid already. No wonder this French gal is such a great runner. And Astrid is the one who is a little bit left behind the others. At the first hurdle the entire field is ahead of her, ow, ow, the Rear Admiral winces. But not so his friend. He nudges Kirketerp. "Watch! Here we go!"

He watches. The second hurdle, the third: Astrid has caught up with the rest, save for the French runner. From this angle it appears that she has pulled even. Maandygaard, excited, again directs a sharp nudge at Harald's side. Astrid takes the hurdles in creamy smooth stride, powerful, dead certain. She is one of the three leaders ... And then ... what's this? She pulls away ... Good God ... At the finish line she flings up her arms...

"She's won it!" says Ivo, astounded.

No way. This couldn't be true.

But as there is no call for a photo finish, the bottom of the screen now reads ASTRID A. ANDERSEN, Vandal (Danemark). She is already doing the victory lap around the track to the applause of the grandstand.

This couldn't be true, thinks Kirketerp. A Danish world champion. There is no such thing, this is a dream. No such thing, says a whole lifetime's experience. And with her awful start...

"Not at all awful," says Ivo. "It couldn't have been better. That's how she was able to attain such a fantastic burst."

Harald is well aware that technical perfection and maximal effort are antithetical. The start must fuse, in a flash, such polar opposites as the greatest possible concentration and the greatest possible relaxation. Well, the Admiral had called it. He had called it in advance, you've got to hand it to him. All right, let's stick around to see the awarding of the medals.

Astrid's victory came in the nick of time for Kirketerp. Here was material for tomorrow morning's entry in the ever-problematic Remarks column of the Logbook. And just in time.

For the Captain had continued to keep his old ship's Logbook — (that was about all he had left of the old seagoing life, a few fat empty Logbooks) — so he went on as before, adding daily entries. Above all, this was his duty. And it was a matter of habit: writing the date each morning on a fresh page and filling in the columns whether or not the first mate had reported in with the ship's data. It was in his blood by now. Speed. Course. These did not apply now. 0.00 knots — ditto, ditto, ditto, day after day. Precise location at 0800 hours, longitude and latitude in degrees, minutes, seconds. This too was ditto, ditto, ditto each morning. Next, the wind: direction, strength, type. These he entered conscientiously every day. N by NE; 6 to 7 Beaufort; strong breeze mounting (B.O.E.) — or antitrade, 4 Beaufort, moderate breeze (B.O.E.) — whatever happened to blow that day. Weather: that too of course (B.O.E.) — Based On Estimate. But that Remarks column gave endless trouble. This is where the actually important items belonged: events, the crew's activities, morale — the prevailing mood of the moment, discipline, confidence, esprit de corps, high or low. This column simply could not be left empty.

So that when five and a half years ago he had been left alone in his mother's apartment at 15/B Bartokbelastraede — his brother no longer alive, and his wife's death having preceded his mother's by some months — he had no more family left on earth, and was compelled to fill the Remarks column with his own daily activities and morale, the prevailing mood of his own discipline and confidence.

For this he had to find the Danish words each day. His mother's death, at the age of ninety-three, could have been expected. Still, his first, sharpest impression had been the unexpectedness of the event. So he wrote, "Unexpectedness". Bereavement? Not a good word. "Being sledgehammered." Passable. Sadness? Self-pity at being left alone in the apartment. No, write instead: "Curiosity. An interesting new situation." And the next day. And the day after. Prevailing mood: cold. He wrote that down, "Cold". As for fighting spirit, the esprit de corps of the apartment — this changed from week to week, even from day to day. In the wake of that "Cold" he felt like writing dittos and B.O.E. for months (and writing the truth) — but this would have been rather sloppy.

In truth the Cold had become prevailing, both as Morale, fighting spirit and as condition and activity of the day, until one day the Captain, right in the midst of the daily Cold, was seized by such an outburst of rage that he began to smash everything within reach. It had become clear that his folks were never coming back. Not that he even for a moment ever expected them to do so, but now that this had become so clear, it took all of his vaunted self-control to overcome that insane onslaught of fury. Now, although the Cold continued unabated, this time it would have been an insufficient entry in a conscientiously kept Logbook. Deliberating at length about the proper expression, Kirketerp at last added, "Incomprehensible rage around noon". But on further thought he regretted the adjective. Instead of incomprehensible he should have written "Justified". This he proceeded to add, so that the entry became: "Cold. Justified incomprehensible rage around noon."

After that he began to think ahead of time about what he would write, so that no emendation would deface the column. The words he came across were written down on slips of paper in an attempt to sound out the prevailing mood of the day. The slips multiplied, his papers became filled up, as were old bills, envelopes, newspaper margins, whatever lay close to hand so that yet another word for the daily Logbook entry could be noted down. One was too much, another not enough, or inappropriate; this one was right, if only he would remember it. Kirketerp was a conscientious and pedantically precise sailor. He wanted the truth, the whole truth put into Danish words. He had never imagined how much time and trouble this would take.

Already on the evening before, in the afternoon even, he began to gather the words, the sentences; lying awake at night, or making his morning coffee, and after breakfast: this had become his main preoccupation. True, he had no other. As Captain, it was above all his duty to fill in this column. But he had imagined a sailor's life otherwise. Discoveries, a new Northwest Passage, the Arctic Circle, and one fine day in his Logbook, the longitude and latitude of some enchanted South Sea atoll where no man had ever sailed before. Or else, finding the vanished Franklin Expedition. Well, it had turned out otherwise. All right, so he went on with the hunt for words. But yesterday morning he gave up.

Gave up for the first time in five and a half years.

That is where Astrid's victory came in to help today. As a gift, material for tomorrow's Logbook entry.

"So that's what happened," summed up Maandygaard. "Yesterday morning, for the first time in five and a half years, you gave up."

"No, that's not what happened." Kirketerp shook his head. "That's the sentence I too had written at first. Because I decided that I would make this one last entry, the giving up. With which I leave off the Logbook, to be done with it. As I wrote down your sentence I saw that was not what had happened. I had to correct it. This is what happened:

Yesterday morning I gave up.

I am giving up for the first time in five and a half years."

"You may note here, Ivo, that finding the words, usually after a laborious hunt, is still not enough. The right personal pronoun, the correct tense must be found, and starting a new paragraph may be crucial. We had our words here; we placed them in a sentence: Yesterday / Morning / For the first time / In five and a half years / You gave up—/. Now tell me if this isn't something else:

Yesterday morning I gave up.

I am giving up for the first time in five and a half years."

"Makes a big difference, no?"

"All the difference in the world," said the Admiral. "The second sentence with its new paragraph; after the past tense of the first, the present of the second, and on top of it, the first person singular instead of the third person: all these bring the truth, what actually happened, much closer. But 'The Whole Truth and Nothing But the Truth', what we swear to in court, is still light years away."

"Granted. Our good old Danish judiciary makes a laughing stock of itself every time it demands the whole truth from a testifying witness. It would be a physical impossibility in our language. Perhaps our courts should switch to one of the Maori dialects."

'Harald is angry,' thought the Admiral. 'We have both been offended by that "Vandal". Well, even with all the goodwill on earth, small mistakes still creep in. But never in their language. Perhaps we should try to get closer to the essence of some of their key words. We'll try that together with the Rear Admiral.'

"It is not winning that counts, but enduring," he said. "But you are aware of that, right, Harald?"

"Oh yes, but for how long? It's been twenty years."

"Think of Schundtvig. What is a mere twenty years, compared to that awful eternity of time? Nothing!"

'That's true. Nothing,' thought Kirketerp.

'Later, when he was already a Captain, Harald had wanted to visit Schundtvig at the hospital. That was after they had heard he had been taken ashore in a straitjacket by brawny attendants, and committed to a psychiatric ward. Would it have been better if they had taken him years earlier? Who knows. Their class had endured the Schundtvig years. They had put up with him, they survived all right. Only two of them ran away, and one had drowned himself in the sea, poor Knut Nielssen. For him perhaps it would have been better if Schundtvig had been put away under close guard before they ever entered the Academy—thought Maandygaard— but not even that can be certain, perhaps it is better this way even for him, even for Knut. Who knows?'

"Who knows?" the Admiral said. 'And who knows,' he thought, 'what they would gain from this? Even these twenty years have already brought all of them closer to the mysteries of a few Maori words.'

'Well, not me especially. But it's a fact that Schundtvig was unable to crush and destroy our bodies and souls because our bodies grew stronger in the constant beastly torture, and our souls, even more so.'

('And that this could have been the object of our training, that kind of hogwash not even our stupid, brown-nose, top-ranked classmate would have swallowed,' added Admiral Maandygaard, also in his thoughts.)

"He hated you, Ivo. You especially."

"Yes, a few of us, those he suspected of planning to survive him. The ones who gave him that horrible inkling."

"But on top of that, you gave Schundtvig the even more horrible proof of the indestructibility of the soul, of its ability to create for itself additional room for play, elbow room, a new dimension where it may exist free forever."

'And what if,' Maandygaard thought, 'what if even now we could expand and enrich our understanding of *Tai?* If, by enduring our abasement and humiliation, our souls learned, in place of our European arrogance, a new (or age old?) humility, plain and pure, one that is compatible with unviolated human dignity?'

'Ahem, ahem,' thought Kirketerp.

'I know, I know. Harald, your hemming implies that it is they who should rather somehow accommodate our European Arrogance. Mine, too, was wounded by that "Vandal". But you know what? Perhaps *Tai* could coexist even with that! Just think of all the possible meanings these Maori words of theirs may carry. To occasionally convey something even vaguely similar, we must resort to a judiciously chosen kick in the butt, we cannot say it in Danish. As you just now reminded me, by referring to that age-old "goatsnudge".'

'Fact is'—thought Kirketerp, as once more he stood in the stern of that training ship, a first-year naval cadet in the twilight immersed in the flawless, unmitigated fullness of daily desperation—'fact is that the unexpected "goatsnudge" bestowed by first-year naval cadet Maandygaard said, at the time, the following (simultaneously, but in this order):

(1) Hey.

(2) Here I am, Kirketerp.

(3) It's me. Ivo Maandygaard.

(4) Schundtvig? Yes. That's what we've got.

(5) That's all we've got. Nothing else.

(6) Anchor chain? Yes, it can be undone.

(7) I see you too have found out about it. Up around your neck, and into the water with the anchor, etcetera.

(8) It's useful. It gives us an alternative. If we resort to it, it's all over. But we can also live with it, with our alternative.

(9) I see you too have figured that out, Kirketerp.

(10) You know what? We'll survive it. Both of us. And each of us.

(11) Because now it is different. (The riddle of the old Danish artillery joke: Why must two artillerymen sit atop a gun carriage drawn by six horses? Because one alone could not stand the jolts.)

(12) And let's get on with that elbow room in your soul, old man! What hadn't been there before. Hey, not that way, this way! (Plus several volumes' worth of Danish words...)'

'Hey,' thought the Rear Admiral, perhaps this is the Maori word for the whole thing. For "goatsnudge". A Greek eta. H. HEY.

*

In place of the old familiar and comfortable "Kingdom of Denmark" the country had officially been renamed "Vandal Sub-Chieftainship," after Marquesan scientists have found out that Kirketerp and Maandygaard's people were proud of their Viking heritage. Their speedy ships had once been the terror of Europe so that prayers at Mass came to include the line "And Lord save us from the rage of the Danes." However, through a mistake, a simple oversight (both names began with a V) it was the name of the Vandal tribe that the Marquesans had officially engraved everywhere. This had an offensive connotation among the as yet unconquered nations, as for example here in Paris. Here, however, as a courageous gesture of solidarity with the captive European nations, they added Denmark (in parentheses) to the potentially grating denomination of Vandal.

"Out of the kindness of their hearts," said the Admiral.

"They can drop dead," added Kirketerp, after some reflection.

Maandygaard gathered from his friend's thoughts that the malediction, for a change, was not directed at their Maori rulers. "Look, Harald," he said, "the reason we can't stand this *Tai* mode of address is that it is usually translated as Brother or Fellow Folk, terms that had been compulsory under the repugnant Visigothic reign of terror. Whereas in Maori usage *Tai* can mean 'Neighbor', 'Kinsman', 'Cousin', 'Fellow Being', 'Companion', 'Countryman' or simply 'Acquaintance', 'Chap', 'Guy', although it could mean 'My Second Cousin' or 'My Lord' or 'Great Chief'. At the root *Ta-i* or *Ta Hi* means 'Born of a Mother'. But these Maori words must not and cannot be translated. If we use all of the mentioned Danish expressions to circumscribe all of the rational meanings of *Tai,* we are still not going to be any closer to its real sense. *Tai,* the same way as *Taboo,* or the word we translate as Magus, Totem Animal or 'Sacrifice', designates something that is lacking not only in our vocabulary but in our way of thinking. We would have had to conceptualize them first and then develop and polish them over thousands of years. What these words designate are composites of rational, emotional, volitional, moral and esthetic elements or units of reality. Of all that, we are equipped to understand only the rational component. They, however, can grasp these meanings instantaneously with their whole being and are able to invest these interrelated contents as comprehensive wholes in the key words shared by their several Maori dialects. Our language is too unevolved for this, and our mode of thinking, if I may put it this way, too partial, too primitive. Can you see that?"

"Well, not really, no," said Rear Admiral Kirketerp.

"Look, we could coin a Danish word for *Tai*, but first we'd have to have a Danish concept for it. And already at the preliminaries we are doomed to failure: our mode of conceptualization is not suitable for this. By means of the rational mind alone, we cannot grasp that higher degree of reality, the way they can with their whole being. We insist on hunting for that rational meaning at all costs, almost maniacally. You too, Harald, isn't that right?"

"Yep."

"Whereas we ought to realize that the unequivocal can never be true. It does not exist. It does not refer to the actual world. Not many Danes are aware of this. Look, they flashed on that (Danemark) again. What does that second A. stand for?"

The results were still being announced. On the electric scoreboard there appeared 1. ASTRID A. ANDERSEN, Vandal (Danemark). "Aagnija," said Kirketerp.

To the applause of sixty thousand, Astrid received a bouquet of flowers on top of the gold medal hanging around her neck. Even more applause, as it was only fair, for the second-place French girl. Hugs, photos. Flags raised, flags lowered, and people in the stands began getting up and heading for home. Kirketerp and Maandygaard were not used to talk as much as they had just now. As much? They usually hardly talked at all except for a few mumbled words. 'How about some scrambled eggs?' 'Sure!' so Kirketerp, amidst a flurry of nods.

For the Admiral was an expert at scrambled eggs, while the

Captain's abilities in that respect ranged from the nearly inedible to pretty awful. But five years and six months ago, when he found himself left alone, he stubbornly made up his mind not to learn how to cook. 'What kind of idiocy is this, Harald?' Kirketerp shrugged. Maandygaard, and we have seen how he could read his friend's thoughts, chided him. 'Now don't you go and tell me that it isn't worth to learn for the brief amount of time left!' The Captain, who after all said nothing of the sort, merely shrugged. "I'll teach you just fine, and you'll have time enough to make at least a few scrambled eggs; that will already be worth the effort", said the Admiral. His own parents had died earlier and he ... But Kirketerp interrupted his friend's flow of thought. 'That was different. You had already been cooking for them for quite some time.'

The Admiral desisted. True, his case had been different. How quickly that jampacked stadium had emptied out. Yes, he had learned to cook on account of the old folks. The camera scanned the stadium, and returned to the athletes again. Next to Astrid the French girl with huge bouquets was weeping, was being hugged and talked to, was laughing, weeping again, completely crushing the flowers in the process. The bouquets Astrid received were still intact. The camera went back to the other athletes, who were starting to leave, then back to the French girl again, and, since it would have been bad manners to show only their compatriot, it cut back to the winner. It took a while to find Astrid for she was on her way around the track, this time walking, not jogging. The TV camera found her face. She was neither laughing nor weeping. ('True,' thought the Admiral, 'he had started to cook for his old folks earlier in life, and that made a difference.')

But still, not such a radical difference. "Look at the French," he said, "they grew up with Liberty, Equality, Fraternity, and they are letting our champion, too, have some of that!"

'And I have a fit,' thought Kirketerp, 'when those Polynesians want to teach this to us ... They are worse than the Russians or the Swedes, Ivo. Worse than the Visigoths even. It always gets worse.'

"That's your theory, Kirketerp," said the Admiral. "But it doesn't hold water. How can you liken the benevolent autocracy of these Marquesans with all those others?"

23

"All right, there is no comparison. But we have survived the others, while these are still here!"

'As far as that goes, he is right,' thought Maandygaard. 'The Rear Admiral is grumbling about the here and now, and with good cause.'

"I could put up with the compulsory *Tai,* and the informal mode of address", growled Kirketerp, "but if they insist on popularizing these (for us) by now long established ideas by forcing everyone to go around on all fours and making everyone under sixty-five spend three to four hours in the trees every morning (granted, only in the summer months) — well, no wonder our youth feels alienated."

"Hold it, Harald, hold it," said the Admiral, looking at Astrid's face on the screen. "I am not sure that we understand them correctly. I believe they have a word for this, *Sei,* which we can translate only as Liberty, Equality, Fraternity. But spelled out this way the three concepts clash. Of the three, any two may contradict each other. Whereas all three ought to work together at the same time, independently of each other. That was the original idea. That the three of them, itemized like that, will not work, was pointed out by our greatest poet, who also stated his priorities: he had to have Liberty, and Love, and if need be, he would give his life for Love, and sacrifice Love for Liberty. The way it works is that these (Danish) concepts of ours may be narrowed or broadened according to whatever priority one wants to assign them. All six orders are equally justifiable, and purely arbitrary. But none of them stands for what was originally intended. If, for example, we place Equality on top, we must then for its sake somewhat curtail Liberty, and in the name of Liberty must slightly neglect Fraternity, which is placed last. Well, you can bet it wasn't this dented Liberty and feeble Fraternity we had in mind when we marched out against the Bastille. I happen to recall clearly that we had in mind the coexistence of all three, intact. Something that we could feel to be a single entity without a breakdown into Liberty, Equality, Fraternity. That single entity cannot be conveyed by our (Danish) conceptual process in the way their Maori word *Sei* says it. Look, the stadium is almost empty."

"But how in the world could they cram these three ideas into one little word?" asked the Rear Admiral.

"By simply never dividing them up in the first place!"

"But why, and how, is their brain more developed than ours?"

"It is more integral. It has remained intact. Together with everything about them, their entire human existence and reality. I'll tell you why. Polynesia's population claims descent from another branch of prehistoric humans than our own Nordic ancestors. Their forebears began walking upright quite a bit later than ours. A quarter to a half a million years later. We rushed things. As soon as we came out of the trees we tried to stand up straight, thereby ruining forever our spinal column which was not yet suited for bipedal locomotion. Ask any specialist. Harald. This way our skull was raised to a more sheltered position, leading to a lamentably one-sided use of our brains, a pathological hypertrophy of the intellect at the expense of our world of emotions. Tools, weaponry, conquest, murder: they came to discover technology the same as we did, but since they preserved the integrity, the health of their total physical, mental, spiritual being, after a while, about eight hundred years ago, they dropped all of those things!"

"Yes, I can see how all this is incomprehensible," said Kirketerp. "For no apparent reason the conquerors, in possession of technological knowhow vastly superior to ours (and mysterious to this day) centuries ago decided to settle down, to give up seafaring, colonizing, wars, world conquest."

"I am glad you understand that you don't understand, Harald. That is, so to say, the heart of the matter."

As the broadcast came to its end the camera made a farewell sweep of the empty stadium. Someone was still lingering at the edge of the track. It was their fellow Dane, Astrid A. Andersen, a huge bouquet in her left arm, her right hand resting on the hurdles that had been shoved together.

"We Danes had also left off our marauding forays, but not without a cause. It was because of internal strife and external defeats after the reign of our King Canute the Great. But we did convert to Christianity in the tenth century."

"That too was premature," said Admiral Maandygaard. "Our

souls were just as unprepared for it as our ancestors' vertebrae were for bipedal locomotion. That too could have waited a little longer."

"I see. Another two or three hundred thousand years. To make up for that now at this late date, we are being forced to move about on all fours. But the required daily tree-dwelling in the summertime, what's the use of that?"

"None whatever. It's merely beautiful," said the Admiral. "In the Marquesas and Solomon Islands they still have whole villages of perfectly built dwellings in the treetops among the boughs. Harald, look at that girl now. What is *Tai* Astrid doing hanging around there all by herself?"

Tai Harald had already been looking at her for some time.

'The heart of the matter is,' thought the Admiral, 'that if we grasp only this much of the Maori way of thinking, that we cannot comprehend it with ours, then we have learned something very significant and essential about the way our minds work. In fact, these negative recognitions constitute the greatest achievements of our philosophy, they are the heights of certitude reachable via a non-Maori language. (As negations, denials, theses of ignorance they naturally spill over and quasi-escape into the realm of a Meta-thought.)'

'But we don't get very far with it,' the Rear Admiral mused, straining his brain somewhat, so that his thought might live up to the exalted naval rank so recently bestowed on him by his friend. 'For in our plain, everyday Danish we are able to express only these few negations. The things that aren't. For the things that are, we would probably need a Meta-language.'

'A quasi-Meta-language,' added the Admiral. 'I will venture' (he went on, adopting Kirketerp's usage to show his agreement with his friend) 'that most likely this is what makes up the crucial portion of the wordstock of Maori dialects. For instance *Tai, Taboo, Sei, Atua* and *Io* with their, for us, unattainable full meanings are obviously products of Meta-thought...'

'Of a quasi-Meta-thought, no? I seem to recall that their word *Ha-Wai* designates navigation, perhaps because in ancient times this island was the most distant point reachable (in ways unknown to us) by their large outrigger canoes.'

'Or possibly the other way around: they named the islands Hawaii after the word meaning Navigation or Seafaring. This mysterious skill caused so much guesswork in Europe: was it the color of the water, the strength and direction of the wind, the clues provided by birds and fish or the position of the stars that enabled them to orient themselves in the terrifying solitudes of the endless ocean? Our scientists might measure and calculate the myriad hues of the sea and sky, the barely perceptible variations in wave and fish, nuances in the odor of seaweed, changes in the behavior of birds on board or in the taste of food; this is the methodology of our mind-set: but all this, I believe, would only enable us to grope our way in a vaguely northern direction. Perhaps the mystery would not be so baffling for us if we had retained the pristine sensitivity of our sensory organs, if we had not suffered the dulling and atrophy of our sight, hearing, smell, touch: everything that tells them which way to go just by sniffing from time to time at sea and sky, without the instruments of technology, without telescope and compass, radar, photoelectric astrophotometry. In their brains the sensory nerve endings assemble and instantly evaluate all the data (including a world of information as yet unfamiliar to us) so that their bodies and souls can put it in one word, *Ha-Wai.*'

'Hawaii, Hawaii!' sighed Kirketerp, 'Meta-language or not, for sure there are some Maori words with meanings unfathomable for our means of understanding. *Taboo,* we have already realized, is not Sacred by virtue of being Forbidden, nor does it mean Forbidden by virtue of being Sacred. Yet it encompasses so much else, right? The spirit of the dead chieftain? Where are we going to put that? Our anthropological forebears' premature standing up on their hind legs seems to have not only set back our sensory organs but upset the equilibrium of our minds. The one-sided, grotesque triumph of reason stunted the world of our senses and emotions. By understanding our world (an impossible undertaking!) we wanted to master nature, through endless activity, tools, inventions, discoveries and finally even at the cost of murderous destruction. But reason alone is unable to grasp all of reality. This way, standing on two feet, in an unnatural, forced, dislocated posture, we could only create a tongue that is totally

27

useless even for the faithful description of one of our everydays, incapable for example of putting into words the prevailing (moral) tone. I can say this because I have honestly tried, for five and a half years, to keep making entries every blessed day in the columns of the Logbook entrusted to my care. Yesterday, during breakfast, I gave up.'

'Yes, you have already said that, Harald.'

'I went to bed late as usual, and before falling asleep, as usual, I mulled over the next day's Logbook entry. Thinking? What is there? For me nothing else beside the hunt for Danish words. Suddenly two came to mind: "Transitional state" and "Transitoriness". I was half asleep. I should make a memo so I would not forget. But I did not get out of bed. Well, I would just have to remember them. Later I woke, and thought of jotting them down in my notes for the next day. "Neglect"?—That wasn't it. "Procrastination"? Yes, possibly. I woke in the morning thinking that what came to me before falling asleep had been important— yes, "Transitoriness," come to think of it—because this was not only the prevailing (moral) tone of my life that day, but of the years past, too. What did it consist of? The daily solving and getting done of the day: getting up, tea, medication, mail, toilet, getting dressed, shopping, and above all, what was most burdensome, eating every day. At least once a day a warm cooked meal: lunch or dinner. I get it done, I breathe in relief, and then—but it was all in vain! The next day I must do it again. Eat at least a takeout dinner. How many times must I begin this all over again?'

'So I think, all right, another day. Let it be. And then, of course, one more. I'll manage. Fine, but how many more? And how many has it been? (It has been five and a half years. I have calculated the days in the kitchen. Two thousand twenty-five days.) So I think... oh, well. Transitorily, transitionally I must do; I must get it done myself without my mother, without anyone. So far, it's been getting done, somehow. Actually pretty shabbily, although I am handy enough, it's been mostly a matter of luck. The apartment? Neglected. (Let's write down that word.) I never repair anything thoroughly and permanently. Although I could if I wanted to. "Nothing is permanent." I keep the Logbook faithfully. My health is tolerable. All the same it is certain that slow, unavoidable decay and extinction are moving in on me. But all right, the hell with it, here goes another day. As long as they haven't got to me. Yesterday morning I thought all this had to be entered in my column. (And which word should it be, "Transitional" or "Transitory?" And the others, "Neglect," "Decay" and what else? Don't let me forget after breakfast.) That's when I gave up.'

'Failure. A bankruptcy sale of words. Enough. I was completely fed up. Just think, Admiral: fed up with my beautiful beloved Danish mother tongue. I had enough of hunting for words, Logbooks.'

"But tell me, Harald, how important is it to keep this Logbook without the ship, without the fleet?"

"I don't know if it is important or not, but I do know that nowhere in our Service Regulations does it say that I cease to be a sailor if my ship is taken away. My profession remains what it had been all along, and so I must keep on with my Logbook."

"And what will you do with it?"

"Naturally I will hand it over to the Admiralty."

"That's me, now. Fleet Admiral Michael is long gone, Alidar is no longer alive. The Danish Royal Admiralty is vacant."

"As I am fully aware, Admiral."

"So in fact you are writing for me, Harald?"

"*Exactly, sir.* And I hereby request your permission to leave off. As I said, yesterday I gave up."

Maandygaard stood up, paced to the window and back, thought the matter over from three different viewpoints. Then he said:

"Permission denied. Continue your Logbook, Rear Admiral!"

'I am not sure, but I may have just received another "goatsnudge" from Ivo,' thought Kirketerp. 'For him, my welfare is not the second or third, but the very first consideration.'

'Now, in any case, fortunately you have *Tai* Astrid's great victory for tomorrow's Logbook entry, Harald.'

'And what's more, it comes with all of these numbers, times, places, just like the other entries with their dates, wind strengths, bearings in degrees, minutes, seconds of longitude and latitude. To fill in all those numbers is child's play in Danish. In our language truly trustworthy things can only be said with numbers.'

'Interesting,' thought the Admiral, 'the way they, the Marquesans are not so crazy about numbers. They barely use them. And how much more they accomplish by having that handful of Meta-language words for the essentials, at least. Perhaps because, unlike us, they always make use of their whole being, their full reality to live their human lives in the given world.'

'Their word *Sei* is an example that we may understand to a certain degree. With a single concept/sense it communicates what we had thought and felt in 1789, but, on translating, as we must, into the purely rational world of our non-Maori tongue, can only be expressed by the words Liberty, Equality, Fraternity. Whereas what we had in mind back then was one idea and not three separate things. If we look deep into their origin, we may even now attempt to comprehend the three words as a single, pure feeling complete in itself without any contradictions, fitting into a simple sense of some other kind of justice, order, goodwill and workable human coexistence.'

'But if *Sei* can express only "some other kind" of generality, then your Meta-language, Admiral, is rather indefinite and vague...'

'On the contrary! We are forced to paraphrase and approximate, in our imprecise and vague Danish, the for us unknown concepts of a precise and unambiguous quasi-Meta-language...'

'It seems to me that the aeons spent by the venerable ancestors of the Maoris partly in the trees instead of walking around had been chiefly dedicated to linguistic studies...'

'No. They probably used the time for further contemplation: observing, musing, reflecting, meditating on the world, to recollect it, think it over in deep tranquility. — Passively, as Observers. Not in constant activity. Acting only when absolutely necessary.'

'And that is what we should have been doing for another two hundred or two hundred fifty thousand years, just like the *(inactive, leisurely, idle)* tribe of Maoris,' thought Kirketerp, partly in English.

'*Yes sir.*'

'Doing nothing?'

'*Exactly, Rear Admiral,*' said Maandygaard.

Both of the shipless sailors could see very well the way *Tai* Astrid, the brand-new world champion, was standing at the edge of the track, left behind in the empty stadium. Doing nothing.

One could read in her face what this meant. Her absorption was deep and uninterrupted. Was she trying to arrange and interpret recent events? God forbid, no. The interpretation was given. She was trying to sink into a deeper and more relaxed, uninterpreted neutrality. Back into nothingness. And to look on from there at what had happened. What had it been like? Where was she now? Who was she, after all? This Astrid Andersen?

'That, let's say, I know,' she thought. 'But only theoretically. And I would like, strangely enough, I would like to be reassured by the Admirals.'

'But,' it occurred to her, 'dear Rear Admiral Kirketerp! Be careful with that word *Sei*, grandpa! Because today *Sei* means: "Fall in!" What your archeological digs have brought to the surface, your Excellencies, all that, all of that refers to the Old Maori *Sei*. And that has all been perverted in the New Maori language, the dispensation we live under today. This word of command is all that remained out of all those meanings. It is now used to designate a Schundtvig-type thing, rules and regulations. (For example, military draft cards are called *Sei*.) So be careful with these two different kinds of Maori, and tell me, instead, my dear Admirals, where am I now? And who am I?'

'You are Astrid,' Kirketerp thinks, 'all right, Astrid A. Not only theoretically but in concrete actuality. All right. You have given me tomorrow's Logbook entry, Miss Andersen. But only tomorrow's.'

'Then, when I go home, the day after tomorrow and the day after that I must continue the Logbook. It is the Admiral's order. There is nothing else to do. An order is an order. But for how much longer?'

Expectably, not too much longer. Fortunately? No. Not fortunately. Because he ought to do one more grand cleanup, by himself. When he dies, he would like to leave a clean and orderly apartment.

"It's not going to get done. Dust, grime, junk, broken glasses, piles of paper slips all multiply as if by cell division."

"You too multiplied by way of cell division, Harald," said Maandygaard. "Just think, your whole lineage of Kirketerps, your Danish forebears, Vikings, Caucasians, back to the Homo Sapiens ancestors and back to primeval amphibians, fish, all claim descent from some algae. Therefore you do too, personally. After your aquatic forerunners crawled ashore and the amphibian became mammal, and human, your ancestors belonged to the branch that started walking too soon, and became active. Whereas they should have kept on for a good deal longer doing what they did before. Nothing."

'I see. So that when the time for standing up and activity arrived they would have been prepared, body and soul. Prepared by this doing-nothing. But what this consisted of we are unable to determine today. Unless it is that point of difference you've discovered, Admiral: those few words of theirs that are evidence, as it were, of the groundwork for a Meta-language constructed of multidimensional concepts which we in Danish can only guess at, since we do not possess multidimensional thought.'

'As for what doing-nothing consists of, put into Danish words it could be: Lying on your back in the meadow, looking at the sky. Or: Crawling on your belly, looking at the grass. It could be blue, or green. Using a Greek word, *medomai,* to think it over, meditate. With a religious devotion. Using a Latin word, contemplation: deep and uninterrupted absorption in observing, reflecting, musing on the world. Dreaming, wool-gathering. Pondering, evaluating? Not at all. Recalling, rather, and going over again, re-living once more, yes. And in complete passivity; what's more, with a passive resistance: resisting the least activity, even that necessary for survival.'

'We are capable of this doing-nothing, and of grasping our existence with our whole being only in our earliest childhood.

And we lose this capability frighteningly soon, except for a few of our greatest creative artists and philosophers. It must be done with all of your body and soul (sensory organs and mind/spirit) concentrated, merging in total attention and surrender. Your brain is not enough for it and special care must be taken that what is then glimpsed will not be hurriedly cramped into our conceptual apparatus. With your heart and brain? That is not enough; with your stomach as well, your skin, your circulation, hormones, guts, glands, lymphatic ducts, spinal cord, vertebrae, muscle tones, nerve paths—they all must engage in it. Stretching out in the cradle you most probably were still able to do it. But it is not imprinted beyond that. For that, our distant ancestors should have persisted much longer at their contemplative/meditative doing-nothing.'

'So that, while we preceded them by one or two millennia in the material-physical knowledge of the world (a function of mere intellect), we were left several hundred thousand years behind in the development of a higher degree of thought and of the language based on it. Are we to start catching up now? It seems a rather hopeless prospect. Much more leisure time would be needed for that.'

Although they could not read all of *Tai* Astrid's thoughts, her face seemed to say that she was musing about that leisure time. A defeat was good for giving a person lots of leisure time for thinking it over. But how about a victory? Astrid was probing it now. Her face appeared sad. She was doing nothing. She stood alone. But she was not sad. She was probing the leisure time of the winner. It was all right. It was going to be all right, she knew how to concentrate and relax.

The Admiral thought about how they had once upon a time defeated and conquered England. The English hated the autocracy of the Danish kings, but their defeat gave them sufficient leisure time for doing-nothing so that their poets and playwrights were eventually able to create texts that are close to Meta-language.

'What's even more interesting,' commented Kirketerp, 'is this news from a distant land. An Austro-Hungarian linguist, Shambocky (or Zhambek?) has recently published Meta-language texts composed entirely in the everyday words of his own Scytho-Hungur mother tongue.'

'Remarkable. Am I to understand that he has managed to express Meta-thought, that is, for us nonexistent, totally unknown meanings, in a currently spoken national language?'

"Exactly."

'So that even in Danish it would be possible to construct and approximate such quasi-Meta-thought meanings as are required for the quasi-establishment of a Meta-language?'

"Absolutely," replied the Rear Admiral. "But may I suggest a temporary moratorium on the word 'quasi'? By the way, I happened to get my hands on a half a page of this remarkable experimental text, as luck would have it, in Danish translation.

STONE SHOULDERS HOLD STONE BALCONIES.
DARK FACES. FACES TURNED BLACK. BLACKENED CURLS OF BEARD AND HAIR. HOLLOW EYE SOCKETS.
FURY AND PAIN ON THE FACES. PROFOUND HUMILIATION...

"Taniwha!" exclaimed Admiral Maandygaard. "The Maoris have a word for it!"

"The *Taniwha* is an ogre living in swamps and bogs, part fairy; it crawls out of holes, something not quite that..."

"And if it touches someone or something that is *Tapu*, then that thing, be it a stone colonnade, is destroyed. Hold it, my dear *Tai*, let's read on."

"What I would very much like to know is how long will it take us, going about on all fours, to acquire the handful of Maori (or Old Maori) words about which, for the time being, all we know is that we don't understand them. And this is what you consider a great advance in our knowledge, *Tai* Ivo..."

"Look here, *Tai* Rear Admiral," came the reply. "Take this *Tai* for instance. Even the two of us have just about accepted it by now. We don't know what it is, but everyone has quasi-accepted it."

"Let's drop that quasi. No quasi. Everyone has accepted it. But why?"

"Because its meaning has already expanded. To include a Meta-thought nuance for which we naturally have no word: let us call it *I*, or *Iota*. We who had survived the first decade of this Sub-Chieftainship with all of its crushing oppression of body and soul, abductions, tight cages, banishments to the unbearable climate of torrid zones, after a mere ten, fifteen years of part-time tree-dwelling and getting about on all fours in Aarhus, in our vestigial homeland, in our remaining cities, the last descendants of once proud Vikings, albeit with improving backbones and a nationwide drop in the statistics of rheumatic disease, but with trousers worn out at the knees and calloused palms: in the street, in the field, on town squares we began to greet each other with most natural-sounding *Tai!*s and to respond likewise with *Tai!* Isn't that true?"

"True," nodded Kirketerp. "That way, with all of us on all fours, or at times crawling on our bellies (as punishment, or voluntarily so as to save a relative) we could pick up an actual nuance of the meaning of *Tai,* something that we could not have grasped before, just as people in other countries where they continue to walk upright, cannot grasp it. This *I*, this *Iota.* "

"And by understanding it, we accepted it. And since then, the mass executions have stopped. In those first days all over the country there were defiant youths and conservative elders who attempted to stand up again, and walk illegally. That sort of thing could only be stopped by very harsh measures."

'I too had my share of that,' thought Astrid. 'Only my sports exemption saved me from prison and exile: a hurdler must stay on two feet. The merciless severity of New Maori is well illustrated by the perversion of *Tai* into something quite the opposite of this *Iota* which your Excellencies, my dear Admirals, have again dug up from the Old Maori.'

'The developmental process of the quasi-Meta-language (or Meta-language, sans quasi) was regrettably disrupted when the lifestyle giving birth to it was disrupted. When the creators of the language decided to leave off their two hundred fifty thousand year old meditation and enter the path of conquest—a path so familiar to us. Technological activities, the manufacture of tools and weapons need only clear rational concepts and words. So that the words of Old Maori, formerly multidimensional in meaning and emotional charge, became unequivocal.'

35

'This way they were divorced from reality and gradually degenerated into mere words with a single meaning until, inevitably, even this single meaning became extinct, a petrified shell. The way for instance the Old Maori meaning of *Sei,* Liberty, Equality, Fraternity? in New Maori (or Now Maori, Noa Moari?) right? is barely perceptible, it has petrified.'

'New Maori, one might say, is a rock formation that, even in this petrified, adulterated state still preserves some of the sweetness of Old Maori. That is to say, its universality. Its hidden intensity and integrity. But after all we may learn even from this. So keep on dipping courageously into Old Maori, good Admirals! See what you can find!'

'Well and good,' thought Kirketerp, 'the only question is, how much? Should we not keep a smidgen of our old European Uppitiness, my dear gal? And how much more should we adopt from our Old Maori finds?'

'In the end we came to accept even *Atua,* although to this day we don't know what it means. Our ignorance has brought on many harsh punishments. At first it seemed to mean the spirit of a departed chieftain; later, a general reaching out for contact with, and help from, our dead. Or a benevolent source of spiritual energy, for whatever purpose. We were unaware of the many prohibitions it included. In some of the adjacent Melanesian Islands an anthropophagic rite still persists in many places, prescribing, instead of burial, the ceremonial eating of dead parents, out of religious reverence. *Atua* put an end to this ancient custom.'

"Perhaps the majority felt it to be sacrilegious," said Kirketerp.

'Not at all. They consider the *Atua*-prohibition a profound sacrilege, forcing them to abandon the departed, by burial in the earth to worms and decomposition.'

"They may have a point there. Not to mention the wanton waste of nutritionally valuable human protein. But then what is this *Atua*-prohibition? There are no rational reasons for it."

'No, not a one. The way I understand it, according to them, disturbances, uncertainties arise in the return of the spirits of the dead if their remaining flesh and blood becomes, in part, our flesh and blood. Their spirits, when summoned, may get confused, tangled up with the souls of the living. That's what they say.

Perhaps it is so—that would give us at least one *Atua*-interpretation. Whether it really is so, we are unable to ascertain experimentally because for us our relation to our departed ones, the conjuring of their spirits, is in any case totally mixed up and tied in with our own souls, regardless of whether we eat them or not. Let us therefore accept this version, Rear Admiral, in the absence of rational reasons.'

"I'll go along with that, Admiral. What's more, I'll buy this before I will a thousand and one rational reasons explaining it as a wasteful prohibition. I am sure we are getting closer to *Atua* here. To one of its nuances, like the *Iota* of *Tai*. So that, if we were able to grasp these *Iota*-feelings after eleven years of going about on all fours, we don't have to worry about needing two hundred thousand years and more for catching up with the Maori language. At this rate it might be enough to begin anew on our last two thousand Danish years."

"I will venture," said Maandygaard, "that possibly it might take even less, say a mere millennium, for just look at what has been produced in this regard by our Scythian or Hun, Hungur author, using his native language (which is non-Maori and translatable) to convey pure Meta-language material:

STONE SHOULDERS HOLD STONE BALCONIES.

HOLLOW EYE SOCKETS.

FURY AND PAIN ON THE FACES. PROFOUND HUMILIATION.

HOW DID THEY GET HERE?

THEY WERE EXILED FROM THEIR BELOVED OLD HOMELAND.

THEY DO NOT REMEMBER ANYTHING. AND THEY DO NOT WANT TO REMEMBER.

THEY HAVE TAKEN UPON THEIR SHOULDERS THE BALCONIES OF THIS CITY.

BENT DEEP IN ETERNAL SILENCE.

SHADOWS SINK AWAY. SHADOWS MELT INTO SHADOWS. A FACE RISES.

A BACK FLOATS ABOVE THE TRAIN TRACKS.

A SHOULDER. A DROOPING HEAD. THEY CIRCLE EACH

OTHER. THAT TINY SPECK OF LIGHT IS SHARPER NOW,
MORE MERCILESS.

FACES IN THE LIGHT. FRAYING FACES. SHREDDED
FACES.

THE LIGHT DISAPPEARS. IT IS DARK NOW."

'Darkness in the stadium. Astrid's face disappears. But we
remember it,' thinks the Admiral. 'Right?'

'Yes,' thinks the Rear Admiral. 'And yet we remember
nothing. They have taken upon their shoulders the balconies of
this city. Bent deep. A back floats above the train tracks. A
shoulder. *Tai!*—they wave to each other, and—*Tai!*—the greet-
ing is returned on the pavements of Aarhus by whoever, whoever
that shoulder or back belongs to.'

'Yes,' Maandygaard thinks, 'we have all accepted *Tai,* we use
it, but let us not try to resolve its meaning, Harald.'

'But even Astrid has accepted it as Old Maori, and suitable for
the beginnings of a Meta-language...'

'Oh, dear grandpa!' Astrid thinks. 'Please don't jumble up two
different things which now are quasi three different things! All we
have at our disposal here is the New Maori, the perverted *Tai.*
From this fossil your Excellencies' excavations may have unco-
vered latent Old Maori components. Vestiges, toward the foundation of a new or renewed Meta-language. Which becomes,
doesn't it, our third item. And for this we must dip into both, as it
were; even a petrified Old Maori alerts us to the deficiencies of
our undeveloped brain functions, while even on all fours we must
put up with the rule of the New Maori, whereby today's *Tai* gains
a component suitable for the foundation of a Meta-language.
Quasi.'

'I see,' thought the Rear Admiral. 'Even I can see that. Many
thanks, old girl. You have solved the puzzle...'

'We, however, must refrain from resolving *Tai,*' thinks Maandygaard, 'or even its component nuance that we call *Iota* among
ourselves. It is very deep.'

"But as long as we have learned it the hard way, what it is, just
about? We can both of us imagine it, sense it, can't we?"

"Yes we can. That's precisely why we must be careful. We

could easily imagine that it is expressible in Danish; we start to do it, and botch the whole thing."

"That sounds familiar. Bankrupt's estate. In the Logbook entries."

"Tell me, Kirketerp, if this is *Iota*, the sum of what our concepts can say about it: 'Total Sameness, yet Total Isolation. Pride replaced by a New Humility. Which is also ancient, the way Simplicity and Purity are. The inborn Dignity of existence, intact. With a pinch of our old European Arrogance, you are right, Rear Admiral, we need that. Faithful, pedantically precise keeping of the Logbook.' Any of this?"

Kirketerp shook his head. No, none of this.

'Many words,' thought Maandygaard, 'and then? Still more words. Let's not try to interpret *Iota* in Danish. It falls apart. To touch it is *Taboo*.'

'That's right,' thought Kirketerp. 'It falls apart, and so do we, along with it. But damn it, how does this Scythian text-maker do it, so that it stays together? He cannot be that powerful.'

'Let's see how he continues. I am telling you, this is pure *Taniwha*! Perhaps your Scythian is even more powerful than they are. He simply grabs these monsters in his native language. He just up and snags them.'

THEY WILL DRAG THEMSELVES OUT. A WALK ON THE BEACH?

NAW, IT'S TOO WINDY! THE WATER'S TOO COLD.

THAT'S ALL THEY TALK ABOUT. AND THEN OFF THEY GO WITH THEIR RUBBER RAFTS. THOSE INFLATABLE MAT-TRESSES.

THE INFLATED FOOLS. INFLATED MATTRESSES.

AND THAT GIRL! RUNNING THROUGH THE TREES, HER LOOSE HAIR FLYING. (WHAT WERE THOSE TREES WAITING FOR? THOSE TREES ON THE SHORE?)

AND THAT GIRL! RUNNING THROUGH THE TREES.

THE TREES KNOW HER, TAKE HER IN. SHE STOPS IN HER TRACKS. SHAKES HERSELF. IS THAT A VOICE SHE HEARS? SOMEONE CALLING HER? CALLING HER NAME? BUT SHE

HAS NO NAME. SHE RUNS HER FINGERS THROUGH HER HAIR.

LEANS AGAINST A TREE.

SHE LOOKS OFF INTO THE DISTANCE.

Miss Andersen looks off into the distance. She is doing nothing. Left by herself on the track. This is their "palisader" girl, Kirketerp is happy. A great Viking victory. 'But what is that expression on your face, Astrid, my little *Tai?* Are you happy?'

'Yes, very. A bit of bewilderment, a great calm, and unmistakable desolation are on my face. Look, it is empty, the arena is empty.

'The runners, the French girl I defeated, and her compatriots all around, the sixty thousand spectators are all on their way home. They all have somewhere to go. Strange, I am not sad. I have expanded my horizons. This way, without anyone, the giant stadium emptied out within minutes, I can see things more completely, in greater perspective. The victory is an accident. I could have been eliminated in a preliminary heat; that, too, would have been an accident, and defeat would have been the same: pure chance. I can see things clearly.'

'You have all the space you need,' Maandygaard thinks. 'You must have space for that, and leisure time. We know.'

"Well, there is not much sadness on her face," says Kirketerp, "but there is even less joy. Nothing. How come?"

"Because she is probing how much of the well-known, plentiful leisure time of defeat is left after the victory, for that all-important, primeval doing-nothing. Is there enough left for seeing things? (Taking care, of course, not to think about them.)"

There is enough left. It is so obvious from the look on *Tai* Astrid that they too can see that there is.

'And what is there? The grandstands, the hurdles pushed together, the winner, her gold medal, the bouquet in her arms, are all left behind. The organizers, the officials, timekeepers, starters, grounds crew and the sixty thousand spectators have all gone home. Certainly they all must have some place to go. The flowers will fade and wilt by tomorrow and will be thrown out, like all the tossed-away trampled flowers I saw at the Chartres marketplace at night, once,' thinks Rear Admiral Kirketerp. 'The gold medal will be mislaid, sooner or later. The race will be forgotten, and by the time you are a grandmother, Astrid, you too will be forgotten. But so will we Danes be, some day, because, on the one hand, soon we'll be gone, and on the other, all the other nations will eventually switch to communications in a totally automated, perfect sign system in place of speech and writing. After a latter-day mini-Ice Age, archaeologists will be busy deciphering what the Danish language might have been, once.'

'And the reason they will be doing that is, that after the total failure of the totally automated signal and communications system, they will be forced to return to manual writing and oral speech, in order to be able to read the tales of Uncle Hans Christian, my great-great-granduncle.'—Even the blind could see that was what Astrid was thinking at the edge of the track. Even if the light was gone. And now it was dark.—'And it will be a great help to have the Danish translation of that Scytho-Hun-Avar-Longobard text, not only in the reconstruction of the forgotten Danish tongue, but as a reminder of what it was like to be a victorious girl, medal, flower, starting number, soul, object— all alike left behind in a vast empty stadium.'

"What was it like?"

(It was a great feeling of calm, my sweet Admirals. The sixty thousand French are heading home by subway, automobile, on foot, back to the cozy family nest. What we too had once. Grandfather used to tell stories about it. They still have those here. But they are nobody's *Tai*s the way all of us inhabitants of Vandal [Danemark] are for each other. And the meaning of that they are just as unable to comprehend as the fact that a victory is an accident with the same value as a defeat.)

*

"I am afraid the child is too clever for us," Maandygaard mumbled. "And I believe we also have been too clever, Kirketerp. Don't you think so?"

The Rear Admiral thought this over a bit and nodded.

"Yes, I do."

"Want me to make you some scrambled eggs?"

41

"Yes, my Admiral," said his friend this time without any hesitation.

*

(It was not a difficult decision, since at Bartokbelastraede, on his return home, there would be no one to cook for him, and he had stubbornly persisted, at whatever cost, in not learning how to cook.)

IVÁN MÁNDY

LEFT BEHIND

Translated by John Bátki

Stone shoulders hold stone balconies.

Dark faces, faces turned black. Blackened curls of beard and hair. Hollow eye sockets.

Fury and pain on the faces. Profound humiliation. All of it frozen a long time ago.

How did they get here?

They were exiled from their beloved old homeland. From shady groves where they walked and talked. Or enjoyed the silence. They and their women.

They were overrun by some vile horde. How could they let themselves be banished? Once proud men. Not born to be slaves. Not born to be slaves. They did not put up a fight. They did not know how to fight.

It makes no difference now. No difference at all. They do not remember anything. And they do not want to remember. They have taken upon their shoulders the balconies of this city. Bent deep in eternal silence.

The sun is shining but no one steps out on the balcony. And not a soul can be seen on the streets.

The elevator is up on the fourth floor. Its door left ajar. No one is calling for it. No one is rattling the guard grill downstairs. And the sharp, impatient voice is no longer heard.

"Elevator!"

"Hey, what's with the elevator?!"

"Elevator! Elevator!"

No voice is heard, none. Only a profound silence throughout the building.

A drab rug thrown on the balcony's handrail. No one steps out to bring it inside. Possibly it has given up expecting anyone.

One door is open a crack. The key dangles in despair from the keyhole. What incredible negligence! Anyone could enter the apartment.

But no one enters the apartment. No one walks down the long narrow hallway to open the door of the livingroom.

Two cavernous easy chairs flank the table. They are waiting for guests. For the people who live here.

No guest shows up. And where are the people who live here?

The easy chairs are waiting for the touch of a hand. A hand passing over them. Someone plopping down in their lap. Sinking in. Once upon a time, whole families sank into them! Never to return from the depths of those easy chairs.

An umbrella, lying by the window. What could this mean?

Someone was about to go out. Was standing by the window, hat and coat on. Umbrella in hand. Scanning the sky. That ever darkening sky. Now it seemed to be clearing up. So, after all, no need for an umbrella. But hold it! Let's not be reckless!

So he stood still by the window. Staring at the sky. Those shifty clouds. That anemic sunlight. Waiting. Waiting and waiting until...

He slammed the umbrella down. So what if I get soaked to the bone? I'm not made of sugar!

And he ran out.

It could only have happened that way.

Or could it?

The man stood there by the window, the umbrella in its black slip cover. He did not slam it down. You do not slam down a classy umbrella like that.

It fell. Dropped into thin air. Nothing was holding it.

The hand disappeared. So did the man by the window.

A pair of pants thrown on the bed. Slowly sliding down.

A reluctant suicide.

But nobody reached after it.

Books left by themselves on the dusty shelves. They always hated each other's company, but from now on...

The floor creaks. Irritably, accusingly. *What's going on? Where are*

the footfalls
the thumps
the bumps
the scampers

the romps
the quiet, meditative paces
the pitter-patter
the scurrying?
Where can they all be?

The mirror is waiting for a face. The windowpane for a forehead to press against it.

The telephone on a small table. Dumb and incomprehending.

No one is calling.

Unless it is the breathless, dusty voice of another lonely telephone. *What happened to them? Where did they go?*

A jumble of papers on the writing desk. Letters, telegrams, bills. Everything scribbled over in a tiny scrawl. An unreadable hodgepodge. A filthy mess. What is going on here? Someone who throws a fit at the sight of a letter or a telegram? Who does not even read them, who does not give a damn what the message was. He just rips open the envelope — and in between the lines of that letter his own tiny scrawl begins to take shape until it covers everything.

A long slip of paper in the middle of the desk. Some jottings dashed off on it, with a name here and there. All of it itemized with a maddeningly fanatical neatness.

FUIT
a grave in the park
Gerald
Bébé the lion tamer
lion bit off her head (but this is not absolutely certain)
Fernando
Royal Vio, small movie theater in the park, fourth-rate
small but not fourth-rate
distant cousin of the Royal Apollo
black sheep of the Royal family
an unmentionable, a disgrace
the general on the fairground swing
a demoted, exiled general
lost every battle
organ grinders
organ grinders leave from here for all over town
Ivor Novello

What did the occupant of this room have in mind? Was he simply jotting down memories? A few memories of the old Park? Or did he have more ambitious plans? A short story? Possibly a novel?

A newspaper clipping.

János Zsámboky: Small Hotel.

János Zsámboky's novel, Small Hotel, was written by one person, published by another, read by a third. Never did three people accomplish anything more pointless.

A putdown, no two ways about it. A scathing putdown. But what is it doing here on this desk? Why wasn't it thrown out by János Zsámboky?

The chair shoved back, the way he left it going out for a little walk before writing. Or maybe he just stood up to collect his thoughts. Muster his strength. And then...

Never sat down at his desk again. By his slips of paper. They were left in a heap.

A ball rolls down the hallway. A lumpy, faded ball. Some sluggish sand clings to it. And a bit of gravel. From the times when it used to be taken to the playground. For header duels. One-goal scrimmages. We are not talking about actual games. This ball wouldn't have dreamt of that. A match between two varsity teams? Are you kidding? Just scrimmages. Plain old pickup games.

The boys are gone.

And the ball is in the hallway, near the back stairs.

But it had enough of this. The eternal silence of this place. It begins to move. Not exactly at rocket speed. Doddering in fits and starts.

It wobbles to the staircase.

Pauses at the top of the steps.

Takes the plunge.

The elevator door is closed. The prison-gray mailboxes. Shut tight.

Smudged scrawls on the wall.

KITTY

  me!!!

Who are you

you joker!
Just me!
But still
DOG
And GIRAFFE too!
A novel? A serial novel on the walls?
There is no sequel.

That gesture is still in the air. The hand reaching out. Reaching and disappearing.

Yellow row of streetcars on the street. Cars jammed together. The doors open, yielding. But no one gets off. No one gets on. There are no passengers and there is no conductor.

The streetcars' absolute helplessness.

What kind of joke is this? Did they get tired of us? I wouldn't put it past them. They always think of something. Or are they hiding? Why, they could mob this place in a second. Charge! And everyone wants a seat. Pregnant mothers. Cripples. The blind. And of course the shovers. Those merciless types who ram through the crowds. Using their elbows and shoulders... And they can kick as well, if it comes to that.

Except there is no crowd.

Even those solitary bystanders are gone.

This must be some kind of game. A sort of revenge. They are going to make us wait. Oh yes, since they've done all that waiting for us. Now they're going to get even. Childish nonsense! All right, already. Let them have their fun. We can wait some. But still... for how long?

The long subway tunnel.

Motionless dark. Tiny specks of light somewhere in the depths of the tunnel. Signal lamps of a lost train. Signals for whom though?

The darkness shifts. Slow undulations. Shadows loom. Shadows sink away. Shadows melt into shadows.

A face rises. And pales. It is not a face any more. A radish. A melon. A bearded onion.

A back floats above the tracks. A shoulder. A drooping head. They circle each other. That tiny speck of light is sharper now, more merciless.

Faces in the light. Fraying faces. Shredded faces.

The light disappears. It is dark now.

The lake is waiting for a glance. For a voice. Someone strolling on the shore in the misty, pearly gray light. And stopping for a moment.

"Ah the mornings! These mornings by the lake!"

And a barely audible whisper from behind.

"But what about the evenings! Or the nights, for that matter! Those shimmering lights... The gentle splashing of the waves..."

"Well yes, yes! But still, mornings are the real thing!"

Peals of laughter. Laughter that floats across the lake.

This is what the lake is waiting for.

But no one is strolling on the shore. No voice is heard. And laughter?!...

What are the trees waiting for? Those shoreline trees?

Distant shouts? A girl's laugh? An old person's cough? Or someone to show up? One of those early birds! Just slipped away from the family nest. On the sly, without a sound. Don't wake them up! Let them sleep! Sleep! They'll drag themselves out yawning, hung over. Stare out of the window. What kind of weather are we going to have? A day for a swim? A walk on the beach? Naw, it's too windy! Especially in the morning. The water's too cold. And then off they go with their rubber rafts. Those inflatable mattresses. That's all they talk about. The inflated fools. Inflatable mattresses.

But she will be far away by then!

The trees understand the runaway. They understand and accept her. But these days she is nowhere to be seen.

And that girl! Running through the trees, her loose hair flying. She stops in her tracks. Lightly runs her fingers through her hair. Leans against a tree. Looks off into the distance.

And the guest of the park bench. Deposited by the night there on that decrepit old bench. His head rolled back. Elbows pressed against the back of the bench. Legs crossed.

He shakes himself. Leans forward. Stares at the lake. At the mist-wrapped lake. Is that a voice he hears? Is someone calling him? Calling his name? But he does not even have a name.

He must have heard something because he lifts himself halfway. But so slowly... Like someone who has not moved in years.

Girls fly toward him across the lake. Wearing diminutive bikinis. White sailor blouses. Cafe waitresses with their trays. Nurses with white caps.

That serious-looking dark-haired girl is almost at the shore.

"You waited for me? Even though..."

"I said I would wait for you."

"All the same... How sweet of you... really."

His awkward gesture. To help her out of the water perhaps. To lift her out. To seat her on the bench.

"See, this is my bench. But from now on, not only mine."

The girl's face twitches. Cracks appear all over. She falls apart. Into small shreds like a torn garment.

And he is back in his old place, head thrown back, eyelids lowered. Ashes flicked from a cigar.

Vanished from the bench suddenly, as if blown away.

The lake, the trees, the benches are waiting for a glance. A voice. A gesture.

And the empty gardens of summer houses? The empty hammocks? The beach shirt flung on the lawn?

The lit-up room by the evening lakeshore? That single point of light?

There is no one behind the wall of glass. The people living here left the lights on when they left.

The room is waiting for them. For the people who live here and for their guests. Company was expected. One of those jovial crowds.

The cheerful expectancy of the furniture. The old wall clock. A country doctor hanging on the wall, always late, always three minutes late. The dining table. The tall-backed, flat-bottomed chairs. The small hassocks in the corners. The slightly murky mirror in that sturdy brown frame. A face might show up in it any minute. A woman, patting her hair in passing. A man, giving his mustache a twirl. Or simply stopping to take a look.

They are all waiting for something.

The clock, to be adjusted by that old familiar gesture of a hand. The table, to be set. The chairs, to be pushed about, while a voice keeps on repeating:

"Why don't we all sit down? Everybody to the table! What's the matter, nobody has the guts to sit down?" (Impatient clapping.) "Let's go! Everybody to the table!"

Finally they are all settled at the dinner table. The hostess brings in the platter. On it, an enormous fish with a glazed look. Silence. Awed silence. Applause.

"My God, what is this?"

"What do you think? A catfish!"

"Come on! It's a whale!"

"A sea monster!"

"It's still alive!"

"Oh, no!"

"I swear it moved!"

These are the voices the furniture was waiting for. The sounds of dinner. The voices of guests.

As they are approaching on the dark shore, hugging each other, giggling. The gravel crunches underfoot. The host is herding them in. Let's go in, guys! Let's go!

But nothing is heard. Not the host's voice, not the gravel's crunch.

What could have happened?

A deserted school corridor. Graduation class portraits on the walls. Antique students and teachers look down in the corridor's cold light.

Why the silence?

Is there a corridor supervisor stalking the building? Who likes to pull up behind a turn in the stairs... And if he hears the slightest rustle... scurrying feet... suppressed laughter... Well, he knows what he has to do. He knows his duty.

But no one walks the corridors. There is no supervisor. Nothing but silence. The silence of stairways, of floors.

Come on! The bell is going to ring in a minute. Signaling the end of the period. The little rascals will rip open the doors. Swarm out into the corridor. Flood the stairs. Besiege the janitor's cubbyhole. Two salt sticks, Uncle Bakos! And one roll! A Kaiser roll!

The bell does not ring. The doors do not open. But of course! Those scalawags are lying low inside. Trying to hide behind their desks. We'll just have to wait some more.

But there is no one inside.

The blackboard. Dry sponge. Chalk stub on the floor. A bunch of keys lying between two rows of desks. The teacher threw it there. He hurled it. He must have been provoked. Aimed at someone, but missed. And he stormed from his table to slap that kid.

The teacher is gone. The students are gone.

Only the desks remain. Those desks have been carved to death. Generations have worked them. Generations have sent messages on them.

Names... carved names... Scratches, scribbles.

Kálmán Fancsalszky

Béla Pereces

The Hermit

László Drégely

Atkáry

A strip of wall.

Love! Love!

One month of love

The faucet still dripping!

Hot dog.

Rose! Till death do us part!

I am a star!

No you are not!

Á.Á.

N.D.

K.I.R.

O.E.

Egyedi, you skeleton!

Golem!

Mamma-mia! Please no test today!

Not today!

Captain Greenmantle, help!

Captain Greenmantle... The whole class prayed to him. It began with a rhythmic thigh-slapping. Thigh-slapping. Stamping. Murmuring.

Captain Greenmantle! Captain Greenmantle!

Down in the gym, shadows running. Round and round, hands pressed to chest, or dangling by the side.

The shadows have disappeared.

And now only the wall bars, horizontal bars, parallel bars, beam, rings, wrestling mat and gym bench remain, left to themselves.

The swings are empty at the playground. A shovel is stuck in the square of the sandbox. A shovel and an upturned pail.

The little pastry chef squats on a crumpled sheet of blackened cardboard. A cute little boy with chef's hat and an eggbeater. Slices of cakes, pies and cookies surround him.

The little chef's smile cracks. The chef's hat is a disgusting mess. Pastry and cakes smudge into dark stains.

Hey little boy! Little pastry boy! What are you making in that sticky sand? What yummy dessert?

Bottles on the counter. Just hanging around, shamefully filthy. They were not accepted. *Did not gain admission.* Now they stick around glued to the countertop. Up above the sign that prohibits.

We can accept only clean rinsed bottles!

The judges themselves have disappeared. Those who did the chucking out. The ones in white coats.

The humiliated ones have disappeared as well. Those who brought the bottles in shopping bags, nets, briefcases, shoulder bags. Grumbling, whining, cursing. *Come on, can't you take this one! Just one more...*

The endless procession is gone.

But the bottles have stayed on in this underworld gloom.

Bottles. Empty bottles.

It is raining. A depressing, miserable rain. And why should it be cheerful? It soaks the roads. The buildings. Dull stuff. Thankless task. *Somehow it is simply not enjoyable.*

No umbrellas open on the street. We miss those racing umbrellas. No upturned coat collars. No one leaping acrobatically, or better yet, in panic, for that sheltering doorway. And no one trudges on, resigned to getting soaked.

Now what...?

There remain the buildings
                   the streets
                   the playgrounds
                   the soccer fields
                   the blackened bleachers.

It's raining.
It's shining.
The stars are sparkling.

The women followed them. They did not abandon their taciturn men. The exiles.

Tall, upstanding women, their hair done up, wearing loose robes. The wind fluttered those robes when they were leaving their homeland behind. It was no easy passage. Those hairy apefaces ambushed them. (Where did they come from?) Demonic shapes were hopping around them. Threw themselves down in their path. Lay without moving in the mud, in puddles. Then they jumped on the women. Nuzzled their necks. Clung to their shoulders. Hung on their arms, swinging. Those filthy little paws on those big, proud breasts. Those women could have shaken them off with one sweep of the hand. But no... they did not move. Did not defend themselves. Their hair tumbled undone. Their breasts trembled. They looked off somewhere into the distance. With their hair undone, arms hanging down, they looked off into the distance.

And the apefaces overran their victims like creeping vines. Winked at each other in snide collusion. Winked and kept up their ceaseless jibbering.

Women on the buildings' façades. Their loose hair intertwined. A chain of intertwined hair all along the façades. They smile petrified, distant smiles. Smiles of obedience and humility.

Plump babyfaces on the walls. But not pleasantly plump. Mud has hardened on these faces. They must have been stumbling in the mire of rain-flooded roads.

For a while their hands were held. They were still being led.

That was when the rabble attacked. Those small, hairy apefaces. Snatched their hands from their mothers' grasp. Fondled their faces. Playfully boxed their ears. Tweaked their noses. Their weewees. Whispered in their ears.

55

You there! You don't want to be hanging on to your moms forever, do you? Such righteous little athletes! Regular Tarzans! You're no namby-pambies. You can hold your own. Courage, my friends, courage!

Loudly guffawing they pushed and shoved the children.

Suddenly it is quiet.

The apefaces are gone. The mothers are gone.

And the children are left behind.

Just like here on the wall.

Downturned mouths. Gray faces. Hardened, wizened faces. They do not belong to anyone. They do not even know each other.

The trolleys stopped. A while ago they still plodded on at a leisurely, almost sleepy pace. But in fact quite alert. Ready to pounce on someone. Say, on an unsuspecting pedestrian. The idiot ambles down the street as if he owned it. Comfy and cozy. Well now he's going to get his!

But who? Who would be the victim? What pedestrian? There is not a soul on the street.

The trolleys' jolt. That last bump forward. Then total stillness. A herd of trolleys remains like that.

A beatup bus on the streetcorner. Stuck. Where was it going? It forgot.

Who are these cars waiting for by the sidewalk? Parked bumper to bumper, almost one on top of another. It took some doing to squeeze in like that. Somehow they made it. Bravo! You've got to give credit for a parking job like that. Now they can stand around all they want. No one will bother them.

The tires slowly flatten. The car sags. The seats sink. The hood caves in. The whole car is one big dent.

The driver's door falls off. A dull, noiseless fall.

The car is only a skeleton now. A wreck.

Car wrecks. Waiting. They are still waiting.

The lions have slinked off. Woefully, shamefaced.

Who could have humiliated them like this? To make them crawl away from their dens? From the whole neighborhood?

No beast could have done this.

Was it a human? But what kind of a person?

Who lured them out of their den. And then must have done something terrible to them!... With weapons! Or was there no need for weapons?

Those lions over the gates. Heads hanging low. Dull copper rings in their noses.

That old aristocrat, corroded black and green. The very picture of indignation, with that ringleted, wiglike mane. Head held high. Stupidly gaping maw.

The others stretch out by his side. They lie low. As if they wanted to warn him. Come on! Stop showing off! Lie down, pop!

The coffee placed in front of him. Not a word spoken, and the double espresso, the French brioche are there in front of him. He and the waitress exchange smiles. Fond, intimate smiles.

The waitress hangs around.

"I have something to tell you later. Hope you're not in a hurry."

He shakes his head.

"Come on! Why should I be in a rush?"

The waitress flits away.

The somnolent buzz of the cafe. It can make you woozy. And now from a nearby table:

"I'm not one of those women with problems..."

That's all I needed! One of these problem-free women! The garbage she dishes out to some poor sucker!

He looks out through the window.

A beatup sign across the street.

KEYMASTER

The keymaster sits amidst his keys. To some, he gives a key; to others, he does not. It is tough to get near him. A virtual gang of bodyguards protects him. Perhaps I could break through the defenses. Have a few words with him. Persuade him to let me have a few keys. Did I say a few? Many! I must get into those apartments! Into just about every apartment. Don't get me wrong! No break-ins. I have nothing like that in mind. It is just those apartments. All those rooms. I must look around in those rooms. Go from one into the next. What is the wallpaper like?

57

The paintjob? The dining table? The nightstand? Maybe I lie down on the sofa. Catch a half-hour catnap. Then up and at 'em!

He reaches for the coffee cup.

The gesture is lost in thin air.

But to disappear like that!

As if they had conspired. All at once, they got up from the marbletopped tables. Cleared out. Vanished.

What could have been so urgent? They didn't even finish their coffees. Barely took a sip or two. Didn't touch the pastries. Smoke is still rising from one or two ashtrays. Smoke from an incompletely stubbed-out cigarette.

An overcoat, thrown on the back of a chair. A pocketbook. A scarf. An open book. An unfinished letter. A few nervous lines.

... I think I have every right to pull out of this show, I am not satisfied with the material, you know very well I lay in that hospital for years and the few pictures and sketches made after that do not represent me at all... they are no good... they stink! As for your asking about my going about in an army jacket and boots, I can only say

QUESTIONS ARE RUDE!

The giant mirror!

No one looks into the giant mirror.

The marble fireplace has been left behind together with that sculpture. A nude with raised arms and the enigmatic smile. The virgin. The regulars called her that. The waitresses used to dally in front of her, and giggle.

No one stands there now. No one is giggling.

The patrons have abandoned the café.

And the waitresses? Where are they hiding? Why can't they be found? Shouldn't the tables be cleared? Shouldn't this place be picked up a little?

Doesn't the Founder have anything to say? Is he just going to look on?

The Founder's bone-white face high up there in the gilt frame. Bone-white face, snow-white beard, snow-white hair. One hand casually pocketed as he gracefully leans against a table. No, the Founder does not have a single word to say. He could never have imagined this, never. No patron has ever deserted this coffee house, not ever. All right, so lately the place has come down a notch or two. It is no longer a coffee house, really. It is a cafe. An espresso. But still. The patrons! My patrons! And the girls! My girls!

The girls, the Founder's girls, do not fly forth with their trays. They do not race down between rows of tables. Or lilt across the halls. They simply cannot be seen.

The honor guard is gone. The honor guard of girls behind the glass panes of the pastry counter.

And those cakes, petit-fours, sweet and salty confections, those French and Hungarian brioches? What will happen to them? What awaits them?

They are crumbling. Falling apart. Collapsing. Mouldering into one another.

The draperies are yellowing and fraying. Torn bits and rags behind the grimy windowpane.

The whole street is torn up. And they huddle cowering in that deep ditch. No one is talking. Not a word uttered. They avoid each other's eyes. They have no eyes. No faces. They lie flat, sticking to the wet clayey soil. The impossibly tattered back of a winter coat. A long, dangling scarf. A shawl. Some kind of shopping bag. A child's shoe full of holes. The foot twitching now and then. And those fingers! Those scrawny fingers! Digging into the muck. Digging a hole? Some kind of den? So everyone can have their own little burrows. Where they can disappear for good.

A discarded can rolls down the street. Who threw it away? Or did it go on its own? It bangs against the walls, against the lampposts, with an insolent, annoying clatter. That noise is the only sound in the city.

There is no one in the ditch. Only gray pipes show here and there. Resembling an elbow that sticks out. Or an arm reaching up. A half-buried shoulder.

Yellowish green overcoats by the side of the ditch, dust and gravel stuck to them. Checked shirts, undershirts. Pickaxes, shovels scattered by the ditch. Empty bottles. A storm lamp. A harmonica. Stone in heaps, large and small. Blackened heaps of stone.

Above the stones, white letters on a blue glass plaque.
Leave it to us! We will preserve your beauty!

Boards thrown into random piles. Rundown and unshaven.
Gruff, bent rusty nails sticking out, or hammered in deep. They
were dumped here in front of the building. The scaffolded
building. They are the castoff planks. Soaked by the rain. By the
filthy, sooty slush.
   Once someone stopped, and stood just looking at them.
Clocks. Time has stopped in them.
   Four minutes past half past five.
   Quarter to six.
   Twelve-fifteen.
   Half past nine.
   Ten past eleven.
   Clocks. Street clocks. Time stopped in them, and they kept it.

Superannuated wardrobes in a barnlike cellar. Tightly packed
together. Grumpy wardrobes. Dilapidated tables. Chairs up-
ended in the impenetrable dark. Sometimes one of them slips.
And the avalanche is on. Then it comes to a halt. Nothing moves.
   Just like that! We were dragged down here. Junked, that's
obvious. But you up there in your rooms! In the drawing-room,
library, bedroom! Up in those living quarters. Where they
abandoned you without any ceremony... In that sea of dust, what
does it feel like? Tell us about it!

The room remembers.
Behind drawn blinds, the disheveled bed. The blanket on the
floor. The rumpled sheet halfway off the bed. Everything in a
kind of disarray.
   The girl squats on the threadbare rug. The boy on the edge of
the bed.
   She rests her head on the boy's knee. Looks up for a moment.
Smiles.
   "Don't be afraid of me. Do you hear?"
   The boy gives an almost invisible nod. Meanwhile he hears a
distant voice. Distant but still so clear.

"Don't be afraid of the water!"

That girl had squatted by the poolside.

"Swim! Why don't you swim?"

But by then he was floundering for dry land. He was afraid of the water.

He was afraid of this room.

Of the street.

Of the playground and the street.

Lovers' lanes.

Park benches.

Afraid even of silence.

And of death?

Was he afraid of death?

The girl in bed is nibbling a saltstick. The tip of her tongue licks the end of the stick.

A book slides off the blanket. She reaches after it but does not pick it up. She remains slumped forward. Her arm hangs low.

Someone knocks without opening the door. Stands outside as the floor creaks.

Someone opens the door a crack. A head butts in, the way a balloon would.

A man is smoking a cigar in the easy chair. He is blowing smoke rings, in a brown study. Suddenly he jumps up. There he stands in the middle of the room with hands on his hips.

Two are having tea at the table.

Sounds of a piano next door.

A cough in the stairwell.

A man bowing on the TV screen. His faintly ironic smile.

The girl on the rug, lying on her stomach. She shakes her head angrily. Her hair swerves into her face.

In the doorway, an older woman. A shiny black revolver in her hand. Excuse me, may I...

The girl's head drops back. She lies stretched out on the rug.

The curtains rustle.

A reddish brown toupee thrown on a chair.

Cheese scraps on a plate. Salami skin, cold cuts, a greenish egg.

The dentures at night in that graying glass of grayish water. What kind of morning are we waking up to?

A pair of shoes in the middle of the room.

One line written on a sheet of stationery. *Karola dear! Here I sit. Poisoned by you.*

A hard, shriveled lemon on the kitchen table. Near it, the knife.

The light says stop.

At one intersection the traffic light goes on unexpectedly. As if, waking from deep sleep, it wanted to make up for lost time. Its red light commands a stop. But for whom? There are no pedestrians. Vehicles stopped running a long time ago. Cars, buses, trolleys litter the streets in groups of all sizes.

The light changes again and again.

No one notices it.

Here no one can be prohibited to do anything any more. No more prohibitions and no more permissions.

The light turns amber. The color of waiting.

Except that no one is waiting.

The light persistently throws its colors. More and more deliriously now. Red! Green! Amber! And again, red, green, amber! And again... and again.

What does it want?

The lights go on all at once. They go out, all at once.

They drop dead. Extinguished.

The traffic signal goes blind. Its light spent. Wasted, all of it. Nothing left. Just a blind roadside bystander.

Behind it, a small bookstore offers its window display.

HOW DID THE PIGEON BUILD ITS NEST?
THE MILLET THIEF. POINTS, LINES, SOLIDS. ANCIENT ROME. GAMES TO PLAY.

Sinister, grinning apefaces on the façade. Did they occupy it with a single attack? Or insidiously, worming their way in unnoticed?

Up front, a bearded old one holding a spear. His beard is aflame with fury. In another second he will reach the women.

Those gentle gigantic women. Actually he could already throw himself on one. But he waits with spear uplifted. *No, this is not what I'll stick into you! My beard! My beard is much sharper than this spear!* For now, he is content with eyeing them. Picking out his victim. He can get any one he wants.

Gray-green frogs crouch below the apefaces. They too are angling for the gigantic women. Low, snide glances. Monstrous, rude paws on their skinny, drawn-up knees. (Oh, these paws will eventually rest someplace else!) Concave chests. Bellies pulled in. But those bellies can inflate in a second. When the charge is on. When that pointy beard gives the signal. *Leave the rest to us! All in good time!*

Letters and a summer diary on János Zsámboky's desk.

Dear János Zsámboky!
I forget now if I know your face from TV or the papers. In any case it was a pleasure to talk to a literary man at the bus stop. I must confess that I am not familiar with your writings and suspect that you write under a pseudonym. Perhaps under the name of Homer. I have at least six pen names, but if I stay in this field I may have more. I have asked my friend to withhold until the year 2000 publication of my poems written under the name of Zsuzsa Lantos. They may, however, publish the letters written under the pen name Erzsébet Holczer. All my letters are intended for the Public, anyway. For that reason I don't always seal my envelopes.

I am an ardent supporter of every progressive and tradition-bound movement. I must admit, I live in the past. Computers and other triumphs of technology—except for electric light, radio and TV—leave me cold. I prefer a four-horse carriage to a Jaguar or a Mercedes. But as I can't afford a four-horse carriage I end up walking or taking the subway. I can't afford to dress in the courtly style of the Spanish etiquette, so I wear a sweatshirt. CB radios? I wouldn't know them from Adam. I have memorized the Pythagorean theorem but do not understand it. Or Einstein either, for that matter. Euclidean geometry is clear as daylight, but integral and differential calculus is a mess. I can't make head or tail of it: if A = A, how can A at the same time be equal to B? It's like a crab moving backwards. It has no use except as food for other creatures.

How do you feel about all this?

And what is your opinion on dropping the "ly" spelling and the sole rule of "j" instead?

Don't you find that depressing?

Please write back!

Faithfully,

Klara Baum

Budapest, Kagyló Street 6.

What did Zsámboky intend to do with this letter? Did he plan to use it in its entirety? Undoubtedly, Zsámboky knew how to work with "found" material.

And what about that summer diary? Why did he save that?

A color picture pasted in: tangle of undersea plants, livid green giant fish, and a submarine. And in a wobbly, child's hand:

The Nautilus was Captain Nemo's wonderful submarine. One of the machines created by Jules Verne's imagination. In his time it was an unrealizable dream. But for us it is a reality.

Szi

SZI

SZILÁGYI

Eszter

This year the sixth-graders were assigned to do research on the uses of water. We chose the protected waters of Hungary.

KOV

KOVÁCS

KRISZTIÁN KOVÁCS

Tünde Bajor

András Misik

Tamás Fleiner

Szi Szi SZILÁGYI ESZTER

Dear Uncle János!

Maybe you will remember me. When you visited us at the Sugár Street school I too sat there in the library.

Since then I have tried writing poems many times. I am sending you a few. Please write a strict critique. I would be very glad to know the things that are wrong with them. Please write soon!

With lots of love,
Magdolna Tomka
Age 14.

Did János Zsámboky write his strict critique? Did he bother at all to send a reply?
Are you sleeping, are you sleeping,
Brother John, Brother John?
Morning bells are ringing!
Morning bells are ringing!
Ding dong bell!
Ding dong bell!

A slip of paper bearing Zsámboky's handwriting.
Köln is offended.
That is all. Nothing more.
Someone is coughing.
But no one can be seen. Where did the cough come from? From the stones?

The sidewalk has heaved. And sank. Freaky mountain ranges. Regular cubes. Spheres. Lines branching out. Meeting in places, and parting. Footprints hardened deep into the sidewalk.

An advertisement on the wall.

SZENTENDRE

For sale: enchantingly beautiful weekend lot. Quiet. Peaceful. Convenient. View of the entire Danube Bend.

Who can understand this?
The old man with the pointy beard has thrown away his spear. And now he is raising a lantern toward the gigantic women. His bony arm offering the lantern. Where did he snatch it from? And

as if his ferocious rage had abated somewhat. He has also pulled back a bit, you might say, retreated. Possibly he wants to hide among the apefaces.

Down below, the frogs flatten themselves even more. Their heads are as flat as if they had been stepped on. They do not look up. They would not dare to. Slowly their eyelids slide shut.

Helmeted women up on the heights. Above the uppermost windows. Above the city. Their faces hewn out of stone. Thin straight line of the mouth. Awe-inspiring severe looks. One flash of their eye is enough to make anyone turn tail. Including pointy-beard and his skulking horde. *Throw away your lantern, old man! Beat it!*

And those gigantic women? The gentle and obedient ones? Well, they will get theirs, too. They will get what they deserve. Their due. *You shameless hussies! We know what they did with you! Only too well! And you let them do it! Haven't you any pride left? That's right! Not an ounce of pride!*

The lowered heads of the gigantic women: the very picture of contrition. Who knows what their punishment will be? Whatever it will be, they will only get what they deserve. Perhaps they will be cast down. Or thrown into slavery. If only that would be the end of it! That is their highest hope. Eternal servitude.

The helmeted women pay no attention to them. Nor do they notice the apefaces or the frogs. They ignore them. They are not worth the attention.

Helmeted women.

Sunlight unexpectedly glances on their faces. Perhaps to point out a laughable snub nose
    overgrown eyebrows
    narrow forehead
    servant fury on a servant face.

> A slip of paper on a table.
> I went out for a walk!
> Out for a walk!
> *Far-far away in a strange land*
> *In a fairy-tale garden!*

Cigarette boxes lying all over the carpet. All sorts of brands, in all colors. They fill the room. They have squeezed out the collector. The box collector. Who could it be? A child? Some little boy or girl. Who would not get off your back until you delivered the tribute.

Or maybe it was an old gentleman?

Or just another lonely type? Exuding loneliness from every pore. With nothing left except these boxes. Crawled all over the carpet, sorting the collection. He was planning an exhibition. Because he could boast of some esoteric brands!

No, he did not want to show off at all. He did not give a hoot about publicity! He just wanted to be left alone with his boxes. He arranged them by country of origin. Then by brands. Or he did not arrange them at all. He snuggled down among them. Oh, ever so cautiously! Never crushed a single one. That would have been unforgivable. He could smell the lingering aroma of old cigarettes as he lay on the carpet.

Suddenly he sat up. A weird agitation seized him. He counted the boxes. One by one. Had someone sneaked in to filch his most precious pieces?

Again he feasted his eyes on them. No, no elitism whatsoever! Among his rarities one could find quite common specimens. These, too, he embraced as he knelt on the carpet. He called each by name.

Peer!

Rothmans!

Cigarillos!

Goldens Smart!

Embesgy!

Belvedere!

Astor!

Camel!

Memphis!

Boxes all over the carpet. But the collector? The passionate collector of boxes? Where has he gone?

The blinds are drawn. Even though they have no one to shelter any more. From the cold or from the sun's fierce glare. The room stays in eternal dark.

Fingers grow out of the dark. Thin little baby fingers. Sprouting like plants. Growing apart. They stiffen and stretch in the air. They fly up. Waltz around each other. Glide above each other. Grope in the depths of an easy chair. Slide across the table. Slip in under pillows. Under the fraying comforter.

Are they looking for someone?

A lightbulb explodes in sudden desperation.
What's the good of that?
Childish idea.

A windowpane flashes up on the first floor corridor.

A riot of colors. Flaming colors. Dazzling red, blue, yellow circles, semicircles, lines. Colors vanish only to flare up again. Any minute now, faces might appear. Faces of former tenants. Saints. Patron saints.

The windowpane glows, prodigally generous.

The stairwell refuses to accept this offering.

Crumbling stucco. Yellow blotches on the walls. A rash? A contagion? It is spreading all over the buildings.

Grayish white spots.

A long white stripe.

Plaster on a cracked façade.

Blackheaded rams. Grim, lowered heads. Still, they can see very well what is happening on the façade across the street.

The frogs! Those flatheaded frogs! Their paws on their knees. Their concave chests are slowly inflating. Eyes closed. Snide faces. They are up to something. In a minute they will be on top of those giant women. Those breasts! Those thighs! And now these frogs...!

That bearded old man! What is he swinging in his hand? A lantern? And what kind of horde is gathering behind him? Apes? No, these are no apes. Some kind of hairy shapes, a horrible crew.

Helmeted women on high. They can repulse all attackers. But who knows? One of them is smiling. Smiling in our direction. If we were to sally forth... Yes, yes... we, the black rams! An irresistible charge. First the giant women... then the helmeted ones.

What are those frogs smirking at? What is all this smirking?

They were left behind in a homey atmosphere. The filmscreen and the rows of seats. Perhaps they were always waiting for this. But that is preposterous! After all they admitted everyone. They sheltered everyone. But then the audience abandoned them.

Empty rows of seats stretching endlessly in front of the screen. They are rather weathered, downright decrepit, leaning on each other's shoulders. Some have collapsed. But politely, in a refined way. Without upsetting the others. After all, the movie is about to start. But what is showing? What movie?

True, more and more chairs are caving in. With a creak or without. A few still manage to hold up.

The filmscreen gives them gifts. Everyone appeared in front of them. The greatest movie stars. The superstars. The supporting actors. The eternal extras. Those with barely a line.

And not only the actors show up. Directors. Directors, cutters, cameramen, assistants, screenwriters. They smile and wave.

One among them stands out. The bull-necked, monocled Eric von Stroheim. He steps forward. The monocle pops out. He raises one hand. As if asking for attention. Perhaps he wants to tell a story. An old old story from the world of the cinema, for this old movie theater. Or he is about to give a speech. Some sort of farewell address.

But there is no farewell address. There is no farewell at all. His form fills up the screen. And those eyes, the eyes of a beaten, faithful old dog, gaze out.

The prompter's box bends its back.

Gleaming dust motes fly up from the stage. The curtain is up. Muted yellowish stagelights from both sides.

The stage is furnished. A well-laid oblong table. Around it the chairs are festive and abandoned. A mirror by the wide open door. Someone will enter. For certain someone must enter.

Empty rows of seats. Empty boxes. And the gallery? Even the gods are gone.

And yet... those thuds up there. A scream goes up from the depths of a box. Suppressed coughing.

A spotlight is blinking.

In a minute the prompter's box will turn around. Show its faceless face to the empty hall.

Still no one enters the stage. Gray dust motes swirl in the air. A whirlpool of dust.

A voice, barely audible yet clear, from the prompter's box. Softer than a whisper. Still, rather stern.

"Oh, at last, at last! Why did you make me stay away for three horrible days? For three days I've been driving around on the highways.

(A moment's pause.)

"I drove to the ocean, many times speeding like mad, as if the breakneck speed could shorten time and make the minutes go faster.

(A moment's pause.)

(Repeats it.)

"... the minutes go faster!

(A moment's pause.)

"Tell me, why did you make me stay away for three days? You know it was torture for me!

(Longer pause.)

"Be quiet! I don't want to hear anything about it! You have no right to talk to me like that! It was no use talking to you. Every day you show up more insane than before.

(Repeats it.)

"... more insane than before!

(A moment's pause.)

"You didn't keep your promise. Remember what we agreed on? You have not kept our agreement.

(Repeats it.)

"... our agreement.

(A moment's pause.)

"Every day you keep saying things that don't concern me and that I don't want to hear about any more! Since you've been coming here like that, you've never once stopped to consider the unbearably stifling atmosphere you've created in this house.

(Repeats it.)
"...created in this house.
(A moment's pause.)
"I'm begging you! Please! It's over! I don't want to see you ever again!
(Repeats it.)
"I don't want to see you ever again!
(Diminuendo.)
"... you ever again
I don't want to
see you ever..."
The voice is lost in silence.

Two sphinxes in front of the Opera. One on the left, the other on the right. They do not turn toward each other. Must be some ancient, deep-running feud. Maybe they are unaware of each other's existence. Smiling mysteriously they repose on their pedestals. Their eyes are shut. They do not look up.

There was a time when they could hear sounds. Laughter. Swearing. *Are they out of their minds? When are they opening the doors? It's way past six-thirty! Is the performance canceled?! They're capable of anything!* And car horns—small, nervous toots or arrogant blasts.

A boy's voice.
"Sakyamuni!"
The boy stands stock still in front of the sphinx on the right.
"Sakyamuni, get up!"
"How do you know my name? And what do you want?"
"Get up!"
"Why should I get up? I cannot get up and I cannot look up. One look from me and the buildings fall down. Everything dies. If you knew how many cities I held in terror! Go away, boy, and forget my name."

The boy can only gape, numb with a nameless horror.

He goes over to the other sphinx. But he does not speak to it. As if that one were not quite as awesome. And it does not hold its head quite as high. Instead, it seems to lie low.

He turns back to the terrible one. The true one. Again he pronounces that name.

"Sakyamuni!"
He leans a little closer. Then, barely audibly.
"Destroy everything, Sakyamuni! Destroy! Destroy!"

The girls are praying. Putting their palms together, praying. Hair braided and coiled, hands girlishly pressed together, they are praying up there along the length of the walls.

She leaned against the tree. Pressed her head against her forearm. With closed eyes she spoke to the others in back of her.
"I'll count to twenty and I'm coming to find you!"
She hugged the tree, as if she were growing out of it. One strange crooked branch.
Whispers and laughs behind her back.
"She's peeking!"
Hey, no fair peeking!"
Her smile was a bit disdainful. What do *they* know?
The sun blazed through her closed eyelids. The down on her forearm was tickling her nose. Her nose grazed up and down, up and down, voluptuously circling over the soft down.
Suddenly she bit her arm. Attacked it from the side, like a predator.
She leaned over the arm. Laid her cheek against it in a gentle, conciliatory gesture.
Someone was standing behind her, leaning in close to her neck. She could feel the hot breath. His barely audible chuckles. Could be inviting her somewhere. *But what does he want?* He knows I can't leave here now! He's calling me now?! Right now?!
Bits of tree bark fell on her shoulder. One slipped under her shirt.
Meanwhile she is into her count.
"Nine!
Ten!
Eleven!
Twelve!"
Her voice is cut off. The count is suspended.
Silence. The indifferent silence of the playground.

The finder does not go to make her rounds. The finder has disappeared.

Just like the others, who had found such beautiful hiding places. Who hid so well in the bushes, in the garbage dumpsters, behind benches that no one can find them.

The bushes flutter in alarm.

The benches are desolate. Have they noticed anything?

The dumpsters are astonished. They will have to talk about this among themselves.

And the incommunicable solitude of the tree. It will not discuss anything with anyone.

A balloon hangs midair. Frozen still. It tilts momentarily, as if to shake itself. Then again that frozen stillness. The thin string hangs pathetically. The balloon is stunned, bewildered. This is not possible! Unbelievable! One moment ago there was the little girl's laughing face down there. She held the string, letting me up and drawing me in. Perhaps so that we could fly together over the playground. Over the sandbox and the slide. Over the city, far, far away...

And now this!

She simply let go of me. Disappeared without a word. She didn't even say. Go away! You're a bore. I'm tired of you.

How could she get tired of me!

You can't get tired of a balloon like me. That girl used to sing when she ran on the path with me. Looking up at me all the while. She even tripped once. But she did not let go of me. She rubbed her knee with one hand and held me with the other. Yes, that's right! She thought of me first! Only me!

She would stop in the middle of the big lawn. The others would surround her. They all admired me. One of her little friends was positively begging her. Can I have it? Let me hold it for a second! Just for a second!

But she wouldn't let go of me. That was unthinkable.

And still!... She let go of me. Left me behind.

All right. The others went away. I can understand that. They were offended, they went home. But not this one!

Who knows, maybe she is only playing a game. She ran ahead.

She ran away from the playground to hide somewhere among the buildings. She wants to play hide and seek with me. And now she is waiting for me to find her. A fine little prank!

The balloon hangs in the air, in a daze. Slowly, very slowly it turns on its axis. Waiting for the owner to return? No, that is hopeless! Well, what then?

Hesitant, it hovers. Hesitant and playful, in a way. I'll track you down, sweetheart!

It circles above the playground. Stops by the slide. But only for a moment.

It leaves the playground, flying low in the direction of the buildings. Practically skimming the ground. Of course, it has to look inside the doorways. It glides over a courtyard. Leaves a bit unsteadily, bumping against the wall of the passageway like a drunk.

Again it is up in the air.

A tiny dot in the big sky.

Now what? Which way?

You know, girl, you play dumb jokes! Others would grab at me, and you...

Others! Where are they? Which street? Which playground? Which house?

No one can be seen down there.

It flies past open windows.

A curtain undulates majestically—keep off! Better stay away from there.

A bridge lamp stands behind the window. It is no longer standoffish, having come out of the corner of the room. Wants news of the outside world. It wants news.

The balloon bumps into a billboard. That has been advertising nothing for a long time now. Torn shreds of posters are peeling from it.

A park, with elegant little paths. No, no use looking for the little rascal over here. No children ever come here. This is a place where couples stroll on the paths with arms around each other. But not now.

A cracked stone tablet in the middle of the park. Curlicued black letters on it.

May the park beautify!
May the people flourish!
The balloon glides past the park, past the streets.
Scorched field. Charred grass. Drenched haystacks.
Now the balloon tilts. And comes to a standstill.
Silence clings to it. The silence of empty air.

Why aren't the bells ringing? At least one lonely bell?
In a small town.
In a village.

A toppled statue near the train station. A bearded man in a frock coat. The Father of Railroads. Once upon a time he sent the first train off on its way. Once... once upon a time. His forehead is dented. Clinkers of mud dried in his beard. The frock coat has blackened, just like that roll of parchment. That venerable document. How tightly he clutches it! It had been presented to him with due ceremony in the glass-roofed hall of the train station. On that fine day when the first train departed. Speeches were made. Toasts were offered.

And they raised a statue to honor the Father of Railroads. There it stood in front of the station. The parchment in his hand.

The statue was toppled. But why? Were they going to move it? But where? And why? Or did they have something else in mind? Something radically different?

Who did this to it?

It makes no difference.

To the Father of Railroads none of this makes any difference. Those who celebrated him are gone. And gone, too, are those who...

So now he lies there by the station near the shell of a burned out theater.

Heavy, motionless trains under the glass roof of the terminal. They were left behind in this space.

Scattered suitcases, shopping bags, backpacks, handbags lie falling apart by the tracks. And the arrivals? Vanished, just like those who were waiting. Not one railroad employee is to be seen.

The loudspeaker is silent. No arriving trains are announced. No arrivals and no departures.

When did the last train arrive here?

Who was the last to stand on the platform ready to get off? A suitcase, faithful traveling companion, by his side.

Who was the last one to get off?

To embrace a woman?

A dear old friend?

Silence has settled over the terminal. A grim rage on the trains. Decay on the tracks.

Facing the locomotive, a sign.

PERFUMES

That is what it could look at. That is what it could stare at, from under the glass roof of the terminal. Sometimes it would go over. Crossing the empty road to loll in front of that window display. Buying something? Or just looking?

Anyhow, no one ever entered that store. The blue-clad salespeople have disappeared. Those forever chattering, giggling girls. The store is becoming more and more grimy and run down. The dingy windowpane melts into the gloom of the street.

The locomotive has nothing to brag about, either. No, not at all. It is only getting rustier and mustier by the hour, as it sits facing that sign.

PERFUMES

Where do the rails lead? Railroad embankments are burial mounds reaching into infinity.

A letter on Zsámboky's desk. Torn and crumpled. As if it had just now been dug up from the bottom of a drawer. It is in his handwriting!

I must know who will design sets and costumes. I insist on Erzsi. No one else may design the costumes. I insist on Erzsi and on much else. I am not making any compromises. On this I will not budge.

So Zsámboky wrote plays? Where did he send them? Which theater? Where was the premiere? Possibly nowhere? After all this letter was not sent. Anyhow, he insisted on Erzsi.

A breakfast menu.

Coffee	Tea	Cocoa
Butter	Butter	Butter
Jam	Jam	Jam
Fruit juice	Fruit juice	Fruit juice

Children's drawings.

How did they find their way to Zsámboky's desk?

An Indian sporting a feather headdress. Headdress and turtleneck sweater. A demoted chief. Had to accept a menial position with some company.

A little old man whose mustache droops. Palm branches grow out of his ears.

An old woman with a melancholy, soft double chin. A little boy is grabbing on to the double chin.

A hard, sharp chin pressed into an old man's skull.

An emaciated hand on the windowsill. Smaller faces inside a shapeless, broad face. Little girls, boys, old people. They found a home in that giant face.

A few lines on a notebook page.

I am reading in a large, white room. An enormous, deep easy chair. White veils hover about me. The door is in front of me. I stand up to go out. The door is nowhere. The hovering has stopped. Nothing is left. Walls, walls everywhere.

A sheet of paper floats in the air. A clean, snow-white sheet of paper. A slight crease at the top edge. Well, not so slight, actually. And there seems to be a tear, too. Yes, it was grabbed by a typewriter once. But there could be no escape from that. A typewriter does not let go of its captive. Not unless it was a rundown, ramshackle machine. Neglected, simply ignored by its owner. So why should it care about a sheet of paper? Why not let it go?

The sheet of paper flies above the streets and buildings. From time to time it spins about itself. Is it remembering something? Perhaps that old typewriter?

Now it flies faster and faster. It almost soars.

77

But where?
Toward distant mountain peaks? Deserts?
Distant seas?
Into infinity?

Chairs look on at the Danube. Chairs in front of the hotels on the Danube. Their guests are gone. No more guests to look forward to. No one is strolling on the Danube esplanades. No one is clambering up from the quays.

Someone is sitting on the steps of the quay. An emaciated back, and black hat. A shadow spun out of thin air. It vanishes, melts into thin air.

The splash of water. The sound fills the entire waterfront. And a deeper silence follows after.

The chairs by the Danube stare at the river. At the abandoned ships from abandoned ports. At the decaying boats. No guests are expected.

And yet, as if all of a sudden they suspected something. Someone trying to slip past their backs. Halting for a moment, afraid the chairs might catch on. And suddenly turn on him. *Well, what's up? What are you sneaking around for? What's the big hurry? Haven't you got a minute to sit down?*

Worn out benches on the embankment. They have nothing to do with the chairs on the esplanade. There is no enmity between them, none really. It's just that they won't have anything to do with those stupid stuck-up...

Boats by the shore. Tour boats, freighters, barges, ferries, rowboats. Assembled by happenstance. But now together for good.

Four lions have settled down on the bridge. Two on one side, two on the other. Are they preparing for a fight? A duel?

Why should they fight? That would be the sign of a most vulgar mentality. An inferior mentality. They have something quite different in mind. They are starting a quartet, to perform chamber music. Only they have not yet found the right piece to play. But among the four there ought to be one composer, one who has been at work on something for quite a while. Then the music will play. A brooding sound. But with an uplifting pathos. But we must be patient. And why shouldn't we be?

The castle on the opposite shore hides in a blue-gray mist. Invisible.

Three shapes in black overcoats roll by on the embankment. Three metal cylinders, rolling ponderously. It must have taken some doing to make them go out. Long deliberations must have preceded their departure. Perhaps they even had a few harsh words. A clash. At last they are off.

But where? What business could they have? What possible purpose?

To look up someone? An old acquaintance? A friend? Lajos Kassák?

Sandy soil stuck into clumps. Muddy water springing up from the deep. Sinking streetcar rails. Bicycle tracks. Houses on the outskirts of town. At one time they were all different colors. One, even though faded, is still an alarming pink. The house next to it is lemon yellow. And one finds blue and pale green ones as well. Superannuated streetwalkers.

The shabby genteel of gray houses.

Flaking walls. Walls split open.

Bricks piled up. Were they preparing for something here? Planning something? Why not. The tin sign calls for

masons
carpenters
mechanics
cabinetmakers
locksmiths
welders
painters
pavers.

But they are nowhere to be seen. No, not the mechanics, nor the masons, nor the carpenters, nor the rest.

The blackened fence of a soccer field. Behind it, the empty field with its measly grass. The two goals facing each other. They used to talk at times. Call out to each other. But not lately.

A touchingly clean, small church. The door is open. But the whitewashed walls are not so white any more. The pews creak. As if the faithful were rising. Raising their heads as the psalm soars up.

In Thee did our fathers trust!
Lord, Thou hast been our dwelling place...
But where are the faithful?
Lord! Lord! Is there anyone left whom you can still shelter?

A chair, down by the entrance of the building. Up above it had grown so terribly impatient. And small wonder. It was not nice, the way they left it behind. Then one might as well be out on the street. And who knows? One of *them* just might turn up, out of the blue.

Doors piled one on top of another in the hallway. Tenants are pressed in between the doors. A strange collection. But then the collector forgot about them. And they vanished like air breathed out.

The doors are laid one on top of the other. Doors ripped out of their frames. The doorknobs by their side.

What happened to them?

Cracks, scratches, loose locks. Trifles. They will be taken away, and eventually returned to their rooms. So, temporarily, they were dumped here in that corner. Just for a little while.

Some joke! A hellish joke!

They have long forgotten how long they have been here. No one has come for them. And they have been pushed out of the apartment. They will never get back in.

For that matter, they have made themselves quite at home. Why deny it? Formerly, they never took notice of each other. Say, a bedroom door and a bathroom door! Or a kitchen door. Unthinkable! That they should find themselves right next to, or worse, on top of each other! Simply inconceivable. A shameful situation. Humiliating. But not any more. A perfect harmony reigns now.

And inside?...

The rooms can still remember. They can still hear the voice of the little girl. That desperately scornful voice breaking into sobs.

"That Zsuzsi! That Zsuzsi! Always that Zsuzsi! Nobody else exists for you! Zsuzsi! That's all I hear all day!

"Oh, poor Zsuzsi, where could she be now?

"Oh, poor Zsuzsi, what could she be doing now?

"Well, now she is going to find out what the real world is like!
"Now she'll learn her lesson!
"Oh, poor Zsuzsi, it's so good you could come home! It's so good to have you home!
"Well, what was it like *there?*
"No! Don't even talk about it.
"Never mind them!
"Forget about them!
(A moment's silence.)
"Tell me it isn't so! Just you dare tell me!
"So you have nothing to say now, huh?!"
The rooms can still hear the voice of that old woman. That wild squawk.
"...don't tell me about springtime! Oh, spring will soon be here and I'll be taking long walks! Who am I going to take those long walks with? Will you tell me that?
"Spring! Summer! Fall! Winter! Idiots! What do I care?
"It's all right as long as you are young and stupid! After that, it's all over!"
Cigar smoke rises from the depths of an easy chair. Evening clouds afloat over the furniture.
A man's voice.
"So you knew the Szalóky girls? Both? Or only Ilonka?"
Applause erupts from and old radio, a grizzled fossil. Who is applauding? Who congregated for this concert? Who is standing on the stage? A singer? A pianist? A violinist?
The storm of applause dies away.
Chaotic gurgles. Piercing sharp. merciless crackling static.
And through it all, a woman's thin voice.
"Bravo! Bravo!"

Newspapers strewn all over the room. Outdated news. Outdated? Nonsense! Time does not exist any longer. But those fillers still stay fresh in the newspapers' columns. Modest and faded, but still... What can they hope for? That they can still inform someone? About some irresponsible slob who crashed into a group of schoolchildren. About a tax evader. Or the future of solar energy. Or some old fake selling his own signatures. New sources of radiation. Yellow rain. Yes, yellow rain fell one day. On a Thursday.

A huge carpet sprawls in the middle of the room, pale and comatose. There was a time when no one would have dared to step on it. People tiptoed past it with timid reverence, like humble servants.

They used to stand around it as if it were a lake. They waved to each other from shore to shore. Strolled around it, arm in arm. Whispered sweet nothings. Exchanged kisses. And did who knows what else.

And now...

The boy has disappeared.

Only a moment ago he was still snuggling in his nook on the sofa, settled in as if he were staying forever. With a book by his side, which he did not touch. He was rubbing his thin, exposed leg, and staring at the wall opposite.

The sun flooded the room. The golden brown summer afternoon sun. The faded patterns on the wall blossomed and intertwined. Sinuous, long-stemmed flowers. In another moment they would have covered the whole room.

The boy's hand slid off his calf. He leaned forward. The book fell from the sofa. He did not even notice it. He did not care. Nothing interested him. Except for that wall. Was he waiting for someone? A certain someone to step out of that wall? Or perhaps a whole crowd?

Here they come.

The afternoon crowd strolls out of the room's silence. Arm in arm, whispering, discreetly laughing. Women in flowery hats, billowing, wide sleeves. Parasols and picnic baskets. Men in colorful vests, white shirts, jackets flung over their arms. They must be returning from an outing.

A black-haired woman in a yellow dress stops suddenly. She turns toward the sofa. Alarm hesitates on her face.

The boy is nowhere to be seen.

The crowd surrounds the sofa. They know the boy expected them. Expected them to stroll out in front of him. And now this!

He is nowhere to be found. Only the book remains where it fell off the sofa.

"He slammed down the book and left. He had enough of this."

"But he knew we were coming."

"Maybe he didn't want to meet us."

"Oh come on!"

"You don't think so?"

"No, I don't think so! He was expecting us! There he sat with his book on the sofa."

"He didn't even crack that book! Nothing interested him except my Japanese parasol!"

"Why of all things your Japanese parasol?"

"Because that was his favorite! I always gave it a twirl for him."

"I tipped my hat casually. I didn't turn toward him, just tipped my hat."

"A graceful bow. Possibly intended for him, possibly for the walls."

"I never had a word with him."

"I never even looked at him."

"That's just it!"

"What do you mean?"

"Maybe we should have talked to him at times."

They circulate around the sofa. They go into the next room. And come back.

"He must have run out to see his chums."

"He has no chums."

"He was sent out on an errand."

"You can't send him anywhere around this time."

"Well then..."

That sofa! That rickety old sofa must know something. It sags at one corner. A veritable cave. Maybe it swallowed the boy. The afternoon people do not leave its side. Are they going to interrogate it? Give it the third degree?

The woman in yellow flops down on it. Grown languid all of a sudden as she sprawls there. She closes her eyes, lazily trailing an arm. *Where are you hiding, you little idiot?* She smiles a dreamy smile. Passes a hand over her breast, her waist. Then lies still.

"It's getting dark," says someone.

The lady sits up. She looks around, slightly confused. Pats down the sofa.

The others are already leaving.

She shrugs, and goes after them.

Slowly they disperse in the empty rooms. As if they know each other only in passing. Some look back at the sofa. But only in parting.

His father had smoked cigars. János Zsámboky never lit one up. Still, all his life cigar smoke swirled about him.

A tattered card pinned to the door.

Language lessons, 14-week fall semester for beginning and advanced students.

ENGLISH
FRENCH
GERMAN
ITALIAN
SPANISH

That downcast horsehead over the gate!

All skin and bones, yellow-brown. The mane hangs disheveled over the forehead. Thin, colorless hair. Probably ravaged by snow and sleet. Sleet and rain dripping on it.

Or could it always have been like this?

Shoved into the wall, into a crack in the wall.

It had never looked up. But what would it look at?

Horses galloping in the fields of the sky? Appearing from behind clouds? Kicking their legs far out. Slowly drawing them back, slightly bent. Heads raised high. Steam blowing from their mouths, from their trembling, flaring nostrils. They disappear. And reappear once more. To fly off with the ragged, torn clouds. Horses in the sky.

While this one stares at the sidewalk. At those stones worn to death. Will it have to account for them once? Where? When? To whom?

The rains have drenched its thin, faded hair. Slush dribbled over it. The sun scorched it.

If someone could be found to comb away that mane! To lean close and brush it away...

Their hands were let go.

In the morning light they ran among the trees of the grove. They danced. They bowed close to each other. They drew apart. Then close again. Nearly touched each other's faces. Soundlessly laughing, they looked up at the sky. And then suddenly these three were let go. Casually, without any fanfare. Was it by chance? Or was it intentional, planned ahead that way?

And the three girls are still in a daze. Somehow totally unaware of what happened. After all, it is so unbelievable. So stunningly unbelievable.

Silence surrounds them. Nothing else, just silence.

All in a blur, they look around. Take another hesitant step or two. One of the girls stumbles. She is caught by her companions. They flank her, clinging tight. They scan the trees of the grove, as if those might know something. As if those might reveal something. As if a laughing face could be seen there. Laughing at their expense. But of course! Next thing the whole troop of girls will come racing out from among those trees. They will embrace each other. Bet you three were scared! And it was all a joke! A joke! Just a joke! Or they might say nothing. Simply take them back in the band.

Well, they can wait till doomsday!

No one shows up.

And the girls stay frozen. Perhaps they should lie down. Little by little the earth would take them in. Their faces, their hair, their arms.

Slowly they set out.

The middle one turns back with a desperate, imploring look. Let's wait! Just a few more minutes!

The other two grasp her arms tightly. Not letting go of her for a second, they take her with them.

Mist rises from the trees. A thick, milky white fog. Chortles emerge from the mist. Evil little chortles. A horn blares.

The voices die away. Only the mist drifts on.

Up on the building's façade.

Two girls embrace each other around the waist. They gaze at each other with gentle rapture. They have forgotten where they came from. The shame. The way they were dropped by the band. The circle of their companions. Nothing interests them any more. Except this intertwining.

And the third one? The one who left the grove in a dead faint? *The land of joy.* The one they had to practically drag away. She does not even look at the other two. She ignores them. She looks up at the sky. Her robe has fallen to her feet. Her sharp breasts point up at the sky. Defiant and triumphant, she stands there.

A bearded giant on the corner of the building. He himself forms the corner of the building. His once snow white beard has grayed. An enormous open book in his hands. The book of books. In it, everything ever written about the world. About man. About this doomed creature.

Who were the ones who wrote this book? Who were the authors? Prophets? Apostles? Founders of religions? Or ones even wiser than they?

Never were their names pronounced. Never was anything by them read. Only in this book. It could very well be that a few prophets have been omitted. What they had to say proved to be thin stuff. They were not worthy of inclusion.

Who were the ones left out? It does not matter. The names are not important. Naturally they were tremendously incensed. They did all they could to make sure no one ever read this book. But this grimy graybeard managed to lay hands on it. He never moves. He never looks up. He does not turn the page either. He has been reading the same page for ages. How long will it take him to plod through the book? Fifty years? A hundred?

When will he reach the end of the book?

That gesture, when he closes the book! What will it be like?

Mountains of wrecks. Reaching to the sky. Mountains of shame. Heaped one on top of another, all those wornout, scrapped

    iron stoves

    faucets

    radiators

furnaces
water heaters
fireplaces
rain gutters
rails.
Smaller hills beside the mountains. Castoff hammers, screw-drivers, cooking utensils. *Tolerated persons.*
Junkyards. They grew out of each other. Out of each other's refuse. Junkyards out of junkyards.

The dead have given up waiting for them. Still, at times they talk about them in tones of ironic pity.
"Well, they've done it! To disappear like that!"
"They don't go out any more!"
"Not even to the movies."
"And why should they go to the movies, of all places?"
"The theaters are full of emptiness."
"The coffee houses!"
"There have been no coffee houses for a long time. It's cafés!"
"Well, cafés, then!"
"And the prisons?"
"What do you want with the prisons?"
"There are no prisons and no guards. As for the executions..."
"Now he wants executions! Can't you see what happened?"
"They moved away. Everyone has moved away."
"What do you mean, moved?! Disappeared! How many times do I have to say it? Dis-ap-peared!"
Silence in the cemetery. Under dilapidated wreaths, under rotting flowers, under the stubs of cheap little candles.

The dead peer into an entranceway. They walk down the hallway. Gape down into the courtyard. Settle into rooms. Open the closet doors. Run their fingers over an old overcoat.
Someone asks... *poses the question.*
"Still... shouldn't we go look for them?"
The others say nothing.
One sarcastic voice.

"And where do you propose to find them? Can you tell me that? In death? In that other kind of death?"

"Other kind of death? What do you mean? What other kind of death?"

A jumble of papers on János Zsámboky's desk. Letters, unfinished letters, a summer diary, children's drawings. And one long slip of paper.

FUIT
a grave in the park
Bébé the lion tamer
   lion bit off her head (but this is not absolutely certain)
Fernando
Royal Vio, small movie theater in the park, fourth-rate
small but not fourth-rate
distant cousin of the Royal Apollo
black sheep of the Royal family
an unmentionable, a disgrace
the general on the fairground swing
a demoted, exiled general
lost every battle
organ grinders leave from here for all over town
Ivor Novello

Jottings. Hasty jottings. But hold it! Just a minute! The author has underlined a few lines.

The general on the fairground swing. A demoted, exiled general.

This he underlined twice. This must have been important. This busted general. A woman must have snagged him. Some little fly-by-night. Who still looked up to him. Who was still impressed by him. Still and all... a general! Maybe she even slipped him some money at times. Did the general accept it? Or did he refuse? Did he keep a few remaining shreds of dignity?

Perhaps this is exactly what the writer had intended to develop.

But he never again got to develop anything.

They looked at the streets. As if they had only now begun to sense the silence. The silence of the streets. The gigantic women leaned over the streets with helpless love.

The apefaces, too, turned toward them. The sharp-bearded old man swung his lantern a tiny bit. He gave the signal. The sign of some kind of sympathy.

Such vile malice in the low glances cast by those flat-headed frogs!

The idiotic stare of the senile lions.

The obtuseness of the black rams.

The rigid, austere looks of the helmeted women appear to have softened somewhat.

The girls dancing in a circle.

The girls praying. For the deserted streets, for the parks, for the city.

Rotund babyfaces. Wizened, gray babyfaces. Broken smiles. Downturned mouths.

The bearded giant with the book in his hands. The book of books. He is abysmal dejection personified. So he found nothing in that book? Not one encouraging line? Not one passing comment? Not one hint? Or observation? Nothing?! Nothing?!

That skin-and-bones tattered horsehead above the entrance!

Pressed into the wall. Squeezed in. That head raises itself. It looks into the distance over the streets. The broken light of a sorrowful radiance in its face.

MIKLÓS MÉSZÖLY

FORGIVENESS

Translated by John Bátki

He lived in a permanent twilight,
as if leaning on a fine sword with
a cracked blade.

(AKUTAGAWA)

1

Long after the train had left the station one sinuous wisp of smoke was still lingering in the air. What a triumphant coup it would be if that wisp of smoke, instead of vanishing into thin air, would continue to linger above the town's outskirts, witness the passing seasons, survive past the elections, the special low-fare weekend trains from the capital, the church festivals and Mr. Porszki's funeral. If it would blend unobtrusively into the daily recurrences of the sky! There was indeed some hope for this, as at eight in the evening the wisp of smoke was still intact, modestly staying in place as if it were simply a cloud formation that had opted for immortality.

His family was completely unaware of these imaginings.

After five, when he returned to the courthouse (where he worked in the archives as a judicial clerk) and looked out of the window, he was still able to see, above the museum and the synagogue—two buildings that happened to lie in the direction of the train station—that same persistent wisp of smoke, as if it had indeed fallen into a deep sleep, into a state of permanence.

Puttering in the archives after office hours formed an established part of his daily regimen. He went home for afternoon tea, as did most of those fellow workers who did not wind up at The False Witness after office hours. Following the snack he smoked three cigarettes and engaged in some conversation with the youngest of his three children. Her name was Ágota (like a lovely ascending curve that abruptly drops off into a ditch—for no real reason this is how he always visualized the name), and she loved to sit on his knee and rock back and forth. This was how at times she came to laugh so hard that she peed in her pants.

Anita, his wife, was deeply absorbed in her work in a corner of the porch. Wielding with a feather-light touch a metal-tipped stylus heated on glowing charcoal, she was burning into a softwood panel a picture titled "The Farewell of the Animals". She had been drawn to this esoteric technique at an early age when, a little girl, she would snatch smoking matchsticks from the ashtray and quickly press the still glowing tips into a sheet of paper, a napkin, whatever happened to be on hand. With some luck she would be able to outline by means of burnholes the sketchy profile of an imaginary visage. A delicately curving scar on her face preserved the memory of a slap administered by her father in punishment for this passion of hers. The setting of the green stone in her father's ring slashed her cheek. Ever since springtime she had been working on this picture in which she was hoping to capture the feeling of autumn. It showed the birds of the air saying goodbye to the quadrupeds of the land—the deer, the lynx, the badger and the lamb. Setting out on their migration were the flamingo, the sparrow, the magpie and the wren. A stream separated the birds from the animals and the bridge that once connected the two banks was now a charred ruin pointing its slivers at the sky. A black sun, cracked in the middle, shone up above.

Anita was a radical soul in ways quite different from Ágota.

The little girl, in the midst of assiduous rocking on her father's knee, would all of a sudden ask, "Daddy, how can you recognize a red earthworm?" Not a week went by without her asking some such question.

In the backyard the adopted aunt of the family was using a comb to scrape red currants into a large china bowl.

They had brought her with them to this town from a small village in the county of Somogy where they had sojourned during the time of the great wave of civil service dismissals. This aunt loved to tell tales about her nocturnal travels to neighbouring counties, about the people she encountered and befriended. In the course of these journeys, in a certain lowlands district she came across that Hangos Ranch from where the family had moved to Somogy long ago at the time of the great cholera epidemic. Two hundred forty acres of gently sloping land: fields, meadows and a marshy wetland in the northwest corner where ducks and geese could breed in a half wild state and where flocks of free-roaming poultry ranged for water. There was a small forest of beech where pigs could root about for truffles. The meadows were full of all kinds of wildflowers, sage and bluebells, assuring an abundance of nectar, protein and carbohydrate for cattle. According to the aunt, horses whinnied at the edge of the marsh in the early morning mist. The entire property was surrounded by steep hills covered with dense locust forests that produced a solid blanket of snowy blossoms each April. The scent descended like an invisible avalanche that smothered the insects teeming in the grass. It was a favorite, recurrent pastime of the family to make plans for a visit to the ranch.

Anita's older sister had been working at the laundry of the municipal hospital for the past ten years, ever since her fiancé died. She had been living with the family for all those years, occupying the winterized attic room. Mária was incomparably more beautiful than her sister, beautiful in and of herself; one could say with equal justice that her beauty was like a flower's, or a crystal's. In her comings and goings, and as she sat down among them, she took away and brought back in her person a constant radiance, a radiance that cooled the instant someone tried to bask in its effulgence. Each day all summer long she sunbathed behind the tall hazelnut bushes, lying naked on the grass in the shape of a cross, arms stretched straight out, thighs tightly pressed together, like a statue gently deposited on the ground, a sculpted form fashioned out of white linen. She resembled beaten and washed clothes laid out to dry, the way they acquire lifelike relief from the uneven clumps of grass. She became truly talkative only on Christmas eve, when she was indeed irrepressible, bursting from one fit of laughter into another; she fairly effervesced in her innocence.

The judicial clerk's father also lived in the household. Having recently celebrated his ninety-second birthday, he rarely left his room and sat by the radio all day long. Relying on his still functional mastery of German, French and Italian, he attentively followed the water level reports from all over the continent. He kept accurate records of these, and prepared graphs and charts demonstrating seasonal variations. He liked to say that the whole continent *respired* in one moist continuum.

95

On most days after tea the clerk returned to the archives for an hour or two and, as his fancy moved him, he would remove from the shelves one or another manuscript box bearing the label of some bygone year. He could pick and choose among the files of forty years' legal proceedings. (The older papers were stored in the basement.) On this day he was especially engrossed in the details of one leviathan of a property litigation. It was a nowadays totally inconceivable lawsuit involving the hill-enclosed Pándzsó district of town and the legal status of the charcoal burners' service road that provided a shortcut to the public highway leading to the woods of Dark Hollow.

Around eight in the evening, looking out of the window of the archives, he noted that the wisp of locomotive smoke was still there, steadfastly in place over the outskirts of town.

On his way home he took a moment to stop in at the inner-city church, to look squarely at the cat's eye sanctuary lamp deep in that twilight tunnel. A peculiar notion, admixed with a charge almost akin to hatred, now struck him. Who could be expected to show sympathy toward something that had perished unnoticed, once and for all, without its trial date ever being assigned?

2

One corner of the photograph was folded over in the old-fashioned manner of a calling card left behind when the person visited was not found at home.

It must have been the older boy rummaging through drawers again. He had recently come into the age when boys are always searching for some object, the identity of which is either a secret, or impossible to put into words.

It came as a good excuse for shouting out in the direction of the backyard, with a certain amount of anger in his voice, "What are you waltzing around for? Haven't you got anything to do?" Ostentatiously absent-minded, Gergely was kicking ball-shaped pebble in the grass; the perverse pebble kept rolling back under the sun-drenched hazelnut bushes. Gergely kept popping in and out of there, a spellbound center forward for whom there is no such thing as a lost ball.

The photograph must have fallen out of the jampacked drawer of the Biedermeier card table when someone carelessly closed it, and it fell so that the photo became wedged standing on edge among the stiff fringes of the carpet. In the eyes of the judicial clerk this minor instance of the precision of chance emphasized all the more glaringly the photo as corpus delicti of unauthorized rummaging in the drawer.

It was an uncertain and rather tired photograph. Its upper third had been antiqued by a greenish-blue discoloration of a suspicious nature that wavered between mildew stain and a marbled glaze, the way some long-ago spilled liquid organically envelopes an object, once it survives the attentions of the obsessive wiper and cleaner. Was it spiced tea, root beer or *limonata*? Or could it possibly be the imprint of a sun-warmed slice of Verona salami? Since the touch could detect no incrusted layer on the surface, most likely the photographer's lab was responsible for the process that determined once and for all the future quality of the image, how much it would preserve for posterity. The corner of a building visible in the photo belonged, presumably, to the south façade of the courthouse. The camera immortalized a small group of people who, judging by their outfits, are about to go on a hike. In the foreground a woman turns her hefty backside toward the photographer; in the fashion of the day her skirt is cut on the bias, while the hem has a deliberately slashed line, as if the shears had dreamily meandered. Her broad-brimmed straw hat sports two wide ribbons hanging to her waist. To her left, a middle-aged man wearing a plain starched collar holds a cigar in front of his mouth; next to him, another man of about the same age, clad in plus-fours, is in the act of showing the hefty woman the long nail at the end of his alpenstock. To the right stands the clerk's father, fiftyish at the time, wearing a four-button jacket, drainpipe trousers and ridiculously large boots: every inch the matter-of-fact hydrological expert about to embark on an official field trip. In the background the clerk's older sister is unaware that she would soon drown in Csörge Pond; here, with disarming charm, she is chewing on her pigtail and cuddling close to her mother, a woman with a dreamy expression and romantically long hair. The mother's hand (with blatant partiality?) seems to ignore the clinging little girl and slips under the collar of the little boy about five years old, as if this touch, this gesture of complicity held paramount importance for her. The boy's socks hang loose at the ankles. One sandaled foot is propped against the wall of the building, in the homeless gesture of one standing about, waiting for dawn at a crowded train station. He is whittling some unidentifiable object with a pocket knife. This is the clerk, at age five.

He studied the photograph for a long time and even examined the back, but there was no inscription. After a moment of reflection he made his way to his father's small room and opened the door. The radio, crackling with static, was announcing melodious North Italian placenames and water level readings. The old gentleman was reluctant to look up, for he did not like to be disturbed at these times. The clerk showed him the photograph.

"Do you happen to recall if they were ringing the bells at the time?"

After one look at the photo the old man pushed it aside.

"The things you have time for... They only rang them when there was a flood, son. A fine old custom that is no more."

Above the onetime hiking party the sky is empty. It could be that the marketplace pigeons chose precisely this moment to fly out of the picture, or perhaps they were on their way back in—and so the gap remained a finality.

This was when the clerk suddenly realized with a pang how stealthily this irreparable loss had come about: all his life he never exchanged two honest words with his father. And for one moment through the crackling static he tried to imagine his father's mind at that final fraction of time when the mind may still be called conscious. He saw water, rising slowly and inexorably.

3

The Porszki file had been missing for weeks. Could he have returned it to the wrong shelf? But where? He checked over the boxes year by year, but found them all in place, in the correct order.

The case had ended in acquittal—although the clerk had his own story to go with it. The autumnal secrets of Ábel Porszki. Ábel Porszki, former land registrar forced into retirement, would in all likelihood last a long time, to succumb eventually to galloping lung cancer. He would live to be eighty-eight, a familiar figure in that small town in southwest Hungary, a man who would be out walking in the streets unaided until the day he died. After his eighty-third birthday he would use two walking canes to shuffle down Németh Street to the Martinkó villa where Mayor Böröcz had been shot to death. It was Porszki who shot him; no one would ever be able to prove it, but people knew. He would sit down on a bench in front of the villa in the muted half-light. The chestnuts would be falling from the horse-chestnut tree—each one a distinctly isolated snap and thud. Porszki's face would be ruddy as ever, his long gray hair picturesque. His mind a welter of old topographic survey figures and lot numbers. And a female pudendum of a remarkably triangular shape. In his colon, the gentle stirrings promising the usual afternoon bowel movement. He would survey the trickle of traffic in the street. People are ignorant; the things they do not know far outweigh what they do know. And somehow everything is an idyll. Or turns into that. And everyone reaches that other one. The only difference is that the snaps and thuds are isolated from each other...

This story nauseated the clerk every single time. And he could never prevent himself from spitting out afterward. That Porszki! No way, no...

4

Anita was in the process of burning the last flamingo into the softwood panel when around midnight the clerk arrived home from the Civic' Club where he went twice a week for billiards and cards. There was a full moon; the garden exuded the scent of fallen fruit, to the music of two crickets. No psychological explanation could account for the coincidence, but the two crickets did indeed start up after the clerk sat down in the wicker chair on the porch, his face turned toward the charcoal glowing in an oval cage from which the handles of the burning styluses reached out like bald flamingo wings. Every silence must progress through the farcical stage of grunts before it can find its voice. The clerk waited for his proper voice to appear.

"Wouldn't you know it, some lousy thief went through the club! Broke into the office and stole the membership money from the strongbox. And if that weren't enough, he goes and takes three brand new packs of cards and ten volumes of the encyclopedia from the library. Kamea—Kitaibel to Udvarhely—Zygote. The illiterate clown. Probably needed them to prop up some limping kitchen stool, if you ask me."

They could hear a mole laboring near the fence, as crumbling bits of soil showered and rolled on the broad burdock leaves. Ivy clung all over the fence that followed the semi-circle of the street, each leaf silhouetted, a silvery scale in the moonlight, with a hint of three-dimensionality which in fact was not there. Still, it gave the impression of the back of a flying dragon curled up in the fetal position, its scales cresting in a mighty curve.

"Oh you matchstick queen!" he said unexpectedly to his wife, and blushed, because originally he did not intend to say anything of the sort, least of all such fairy-tale sentimentality. The clerk was conscious of the murky shadows where even words crawled all over each other like caterpillars, unable to distinguish each other's gender or kind—mere potentialities in the antechamber of speech.

"Aren't you afraid that by the time you are done with it…"

"I try not to think about that. I still can't quite see the precise movement of the deer, the way it turns to look back at the charred

101

bridge. That too is a real problem, trying to depict charring by means of charring. Because I have to use fire too. It's a real dilemma. Little Andris today looked back from the garden gate... Perhaps he will help me find the gesture I am looking for."

"You are going to finish this and perhaps something else is going to be finished as well. Who knows?"

"You think it has that much power? I think you overestimate it. I would simply like to express myself."

"To express or repress?"

"Why are you such a grouch? Did that theft upset you?"

"It was not at our house."

"If you want to know the truth, I am still smarting from that slap long ago. The way it split my skin and bloodied the emerald ring. I've never told this to anyone, but once I had a nightmare about it, that my period came, when I was seven..."

"Haven't you ever noticed that we never fry chicken's blood with chopped onions?"

Anita started to laugh.

"That's right! Much to Aunt Iduska's dismay. She claims that is the ultimate delicacy at the Hangos Ranch."

"Isn't she traveling tonight? It is a full moon."

"So far it's been quiet."

"She doesn't make that much noise..."

The aunt had a special fondness for traveling on moonlit nights. She would lay out her ruffled, blue calico dress by the bedside, while she was overcome by something like a panic of benevolence and hopeful expectation.

The mole limped lazily across the gravelly path.

"We might be getting gray squirrels in the attic," he went on, lighting a cigarette on a live coal. "Then we're in for trouble upstairs."

"Mária would have told us if they kept her up at night. She hasn't mentioned a thing."

"She has, to me."

"You're saying that as if you'd just made it up. You'll never know how grateful she is for living here with us."

"I do too, I know how good the two of you are to each other.

It's almost as if when you lost your virginity you lost it on her behalf, too."

Anita, picking up two burning sticks at the same time, with the utmost delicacy singed into the wood panel the flamingo's beak, a neat cuneiform.

Throughout the entire conversation she had been waiting for this slow-motion moment when she would feel in her fingertips the precise shape of the one and only possible line. The medium had no room for hesitation or second thoughts—as if it were the exact opposite of forgiveness.

"The joke is that even these two-bit thieves end up in boxes in the archive," said the clerk with a yawn.

Then, after a short pause:

"Shouldn't I look around in the attic? I could put down some rat poison."

"Don't you go up there. You would wake up Mária." She removed her sticks from the glowing embers. "I am calling it a day. Is tomorrow Friday?"

The clerk consulted his watch.

"We are a little ways into Friday already..."

It could have been an illustration straight from the Porszki story, the way the ripe fruit kept falling in the garden, with distinct, isolated thuds.

5

Strangely enough, the wisp of smoke anchored over the outskirts did not create much of a stir in town. Since its appearance scores of trains have departed from the station, their smoke dispersing in the customary manner; this one, however, stayed on, etched once and for all into the sky. People no doubt saw it, but they simply failed to pay attention. For instance they forgot to remark how at sunrise (for the wisp of smoke floated to the east) the sun's rays did not actually pierce it but outlined its edges in radiantly sharp contour, as if it were a rock reef lying off in the ocean's blue distance. Not unsurprisingly, to the casual observer this formation seemed merely a part of the endless procession of clouds, now lagging behind and now leading the pack, so that it was no more exceptional than a love child in a prolific family teeming with children. And anyway, there was no shortage of truly sensational news, in addition to the expectable summertime hoaxes. On the fourteenth of July a young woman's body was found in the middle of the wheatfield near the Bazsó ranch. The body was discovered by the pilot of an agricultural airplane early in the morning. He was on the way to work; the sun happened to be directly in his line of flight so that the nose of the airplane seemed to be pointing at it. He flew over an enormous field of wheat that stood tall everywhere, stems swaying without a break; their ceaseless motion rendered the land's contours wavering and uncertain. Only the empty blue sky offered a secure foothold. Birds must feel this way, scudding windblown in a rainless storm, trusting their bodies to the buttery smooth speed that could at the same time pass for the most perfect stillness, as down below leafy boughs boil whipped by the tempest, everything whirls and rages, setting the stage for the collapse of one suddenly arising abyss into another, while through momentary gaps in the frenzied leafage madly dashing animals flash by like shipwrecked bodies tossed about before being swallowed by the waves. On this morning the wheatfields of Saponya were rippling like a smooth caress. All of a sudden the following sight confronted the pilot's eyes: in a circle of nearly fifty meters' radius the wheat lay in twisted heaps upon the ground, as if a towering whirlwind had swooped from on high, a skyscraper tornado, a gigantic spinning top. In the middle of the flattened wheat lay the dead woman. Her arms were flung straight out in the style of a cross; her thighs were tightly pressed together. The dress she wore was snow-white. Only the hem of her skirt was decorated, edged as it were by a strip of aquamarine polka dots of various sizes. The pilot circled above her for some moments in total confusion. At last he passed so low over her that the woman's long hair rose in the rush of air which also pulled her skirt up to her waist. A sudden flush of shame made the pilot go through several maneuvers until he at last succeeded in blowing the skirt back in place. He immediately returned to his home base to file a report. The mysterious tragedy made front-page news. At the suggestion of the chief of police aerial photographs of the scene were taken before the removal of the body. The picture published in the Sunday supplement was such a successful photograph, it had such stunning esthetic effects on the viewer that many people clipped it out to pin it on the wall. At the Casino there were detailed analyses of the magic atmosphere of the photograph, its masterful composition. The general opinion was that something like this could not be made up: it was one of those things that could only happen in real life. The wheat had been flattened in an area that was almost a perfect circle, and its chaotic disarray had a frozen calm compared to which any imagined order appeared to be a mere exercise in futility. Yes indeed, they said, perhaps the things we mean by our notion of decay belong in actuality to a more complicated category, a world order beyond our ken. And the fact of that recumbent female body in the face of all logic!—artistic and gracefully morbid, ethereal and weighing a ton, whereas the surrounding space—it was pointed out—seemed like the crushed petals of a giant flower with an anthropomorphic pistil spreading its arms in the center! An image verging on mysteries. Especially when you consider that remarkable lack of transition—one of the characteristics of naive art—in the way the disheveled area is enclosed by the solid mass of the field of standing wheat, a wall sturdier than a billion spiky infantrymen ready for deployment in action. This fantastic contrast had an especially powerful esthetic magic of its own, it was said. A stage without entrance or exit. Regarding this, the

105

observant reader and beholder had every right to be further confused by the fact that after the most painstaking perusal of the aerial photo police investigators were unable to find in the wheatfield around the scene the mysterious track, no matter how tenuous, that would have been made by someone approaching the victim—so that she could be gently strangled (possibly while asleep?). Or else, how did the victim get to the spot where she lay, and what was the manner of her death?

6

Around this time Mária had a dream (almost as if she had continued weaving Anita's recurrent dream):

Wearing a red dress she stepped into a muddy lake; the turbid water soaked through the dress, making the red darker. Like black blood, it seeped through her white undergarment. Above the lake, tracing the arc of an invisible rainbow, a white baby carriage rolled across the sky.

The following morning her period arrived unexpectedly.

7

Weeks later the Porszki file turned up again. The dossier had an addendum attached to it, consisting of several pages of depositions by witnesses, a four-column newspaper clipping, a sketchy map of the Pándzsó district in earlier times, and an itemized list of archival documents containing references of whatever nature to the town magistrate Ádám Böröcz. The clerk's attention was immediately drawn to the newspaper article, authored by one Syrasius Acrotophorius, which had appeared in the literary columns of the county paper, some months before the trial in 1922. (The *nom de plume* presumably hid the identity of the pseudonymous county laureate Jakab Mariosa, who had a predilection for romantic themes borrowed from the town's past; according to his obituary, he died of consumption, but local rumour maintained that he was strangled in retribution for an indiscreet *roman à clef*. But his colorful historical phantasmagorias enjoyed great popularity in the inflationary years following the war.)

Syrasius Acrotophorius limned a picturesque image of the Pándzsó in olden days. He even made reference to the disputed service road of the charcoal burners which, according to oral tradition, passed near the site of the *necropolis*. Indeed, this burial ground was no mere figment of the imagination; written references pointed to its existence and an abundance of bones had been dug up, although the possibility still remained that the references (and map) may have been phantasmagoria in their own day; (we are speaking of the 1600s). The map was eventually published in the local historical yearbook; it was discussed and analyzed, but no definite conclusions were reached. Acrotophorius patched his tale together out of various conjectures, and titled his piece, most suggestively, "Churchflood". The town's churchbells used to be sounded twice each noontime: once for the salvation of the living and once for the salvation of the dead. The loud tolling of bells—he tells us—disrupted the silence of spiral staircases, drowned out the resonant organ pipes, the creaking of the belfry and the noise of the crowd gathered in the church piazza. Assembling there for the pealing of the bells was a local custom. Old folks, ragamuffins, street urchins, epileptics with their hair braided into knots, or bearing the bald spots of old scars, out-of-towners, speakers of foreign languages (most of them from the Balkans, swept this far by the Turks), prisoners of other customs until mercy and tolerance went to work on them and herded them together, or rather, loneliness did, or more precisely, fear, or still more precisely, a desperation that was ready to do anything (if need be) — but all this was not apparent during the tolling of the bells, which was only a signal, clear and independent of these people; the bronze behemoths were still capable of that, and perhaps precisely this constituted their aristocratic irony, an irony *in saeculo saeculorum*. The booming tones rolled reverberating over the steeples, crosses and crescents of the small town huddled close to the green range of hills, and jammed into the alleyways, where the sounds backed up, like air too thick to breathe in for weak chests, and had to rush back out again under the arcades. In those days the Pándzsó district lay at a greater distance from the center of town, so that only the outermost edge of the tintinnabulation would reach that far, the way the tip of a windblown branch keeps brushing against a wall. That was where a labyrinthine mass grave was dug for victims of the plague, in nine parcels corresponding to the nine town districts, and with a miniature arrangement of the placement and orientation of the town's streets, so that the bodies, marked by numbers, could be thrown into the same district and street they had inhabited in their lifetime. Tradition links this scheme to the name of the town magistrate Böröcz. Acrotophorius goes on to provide further details. The town took so much civic pride in imposing the same kind of order on its replica as on the original that an accurately drawn map of the necropolis was commisioned. (One of the sketches may be seen at the archive.) For nine months a register recorded the daily increment of the population, noting the deceased's occupation, financial standing, titles and honors, family status, police record, if any, religious affiliation, and if the family died out, the amount of taxes owed. A copy of these records and annotations was locked up in a lead casket and buried in the middle of the seventh parcel at the site corresponding to the "town hall". Probably it is still there to this day. And at this point the narrative really takes a leap. In the course of time this same Pándzsó district became the traditional setting for the Plague Festival and the Plague Fast that followed. Each lasted for three days, but the preparations took weeks. That was how long it took to create the fantastic masks and costumes representing the plague victims, and to commit to memory every single detail preserved by family tradition about the deceased: minutiae of their personal lives and public affairs, even their "presumable feelings and thoughts". A specially appointed Festival Committee dealt with all of these matters. For membership on the committee the lower age limit was three years, and as there was no upper limit, the authenticity of the reconstructions could be ascertained as thoroughly as possible. The committee took all things into consideration and kept records of everything: oral tradition, hearsay, family archives, descendants' atavistic mannerisms, slips of the tongue, dreams, habits, accents, unexpected and recurrent déjà vus. Year by year they assembled the same image, although in a different form, of every plague victim: different, because the people who at festival time donned the masks and participated in the "reconstruction workshops" were after all not the same from year to year. Preparations for the Festival also meant the construction of the Ogre. Anyone could participate in this enterprise, local citizens as well as strangers who flocked to the town. Ideas and suggestions of whatever nature were legitimate, allowable, solicited and expected; after all, the Ogre belonged to everyone, it was an unpredictable, forever fresh surprise, communal terror, vision, general confession, cackling, exhibitionism, profound corruption, pornography, open-air mass. The Ogre was erected on the town's main square on a rough timber foundation measuring seven by seven meters equipped on two sides with iron-shod wheels sawed from treetrunks; the whole contraption was dragged on the day of the Festival to the Pándzsó. While the Ogre was under construction sexual abstinence was the rule, but this did not preclude a preoccupation with sexuality. During this season the streets and alleyways rang out with gushing outpourings, sudden raw propositions, totally unrestrained squirmings, scream answering scream in the dead of night, touchie-feelie euphorias, misty-eyed reveries, quivery jumpiness, wide-awake swoons, glassy-eyed stares, languid language, sweaty silence, petrified pantings, splattering death leaps, rock-still quiet...

In his article Acrotophorius boldly asserts that he has found the historical precedents, hitherto unknown, of the festival masquerades. Porszki's defense lawyer argued that this "turgid horror story" provided the unfortunate grounds for a whisper campaign associating his client's name with the murder. As it turned out the town magistrate Böröcz—and this was a well-attested fact—had once denied the vintner Vencel (one of the Porszki ancestors) the right to a decent burial in the bosom of his family, because he had been in prison at the outbreak of the pestilence. (He had been caught in the act of *bestiality;* according to the court records he had carnal relations with a cow on six occasions *"contra naturalem usum, an gehörigen Orthe gebraucht hate"*, on two of these occasions in a sober state and always with the same cow, by the accused's own admission.) In the end the plague carried him off and he was thrown into a pit outside of the bounds of the necropolis. The case would have remained a mere curiosity had it not been for the fact that the mayor's father, at the time of the 1896 Millennial masquerades—and could this have been some crude reminder of the past?—rode around on a cow to serenade the land registrar's mother. And so the rift between the two families was again deepened.

A revenge, centuries in the making?

It was late at night when the clerk finished his perusal of the file. For some unknown reason the revulsion he had always felt for Porszki was now diluted by a certain titivated curiosity. Porszki! Still, no way, no...

The town was bathed in moonlight. The wisp of smoke, like a glimmering tapestry fragment, lay low, friendly and self-effacing among the other stage props.

8

One day in early August Anita came home from the marketplace in a most agitated state. As usual, she had taken with her Gergely's rubber-tired wagon which she loaded with ten pounds of red potatoes, several secretive-faced celery roots, some shortneck Bosc pears, strident bunches of white icicle radishes and baby carrots that emitted a moist yellow light like the pallor of deep-sea fish. And other wondrous produce of the land. All of this probably involved a simpler rite back at the Hangos Ranch, where the humus was worked through and through by busy earthworms so that everything cropped up straight from that; there the dew coated the leaves like a crystalline rash, and when a vegetable was pulled out of the soil the girls would call the gaping wound it left behind by some other name.

A slow lukewarm drizzle caught up with her in Németh Street. The first thing she noticed was a soft susurrus, and, as when a transparency is slid into a projector, this was immediately followed by the image so familiar to her eyes: the jogging girls from the secondary school approaching behind her with the muffled patter of their sneakers, progressing along Németh Street to turn around at the hospital chapel—the usual course of their morning warmup run. Whereas in actuality she merely happened to catch that rare moment when the rain's line of advance trails one like some lackadaisical hound, always managing to stay just behind one's back. The subdued chords of a piano, a Chopin étude, issued from the house next to the Martinkó villa. The rain and the music combined into a harmonious whole. The sudden ambience of a gossamer memory fragment caught Anita by surprise, but it was a memory without any substance; it merely imbued the image of the street with an unusual poignance. The windows of this building did not align in parallel with the level of the sidewalk; the two lines were at a slight angle, leaving the meeting point of their extensions in abeyance, somewhere off in the distance. This symmetry, too, now seemed to identify somehow with the memory fragment, without actually forming its subject. This was what Anita became oblivious to the instant a black mongrel dog squeezed out of the cement-ringed drainpipe of the house, its hair slimy with iridescent sewage, in its frantic rush toward the chapel the mongrel upset the shopping cart. At the same moment the elderly Miss Farda appeared at one of the windows and shouted.

"Somebody drown that cur!"

An embroidered handkerchief flashed white in her hand.

When she saw the scattered groceries, she quickly disappeared from view.

Anita arrived home soaked to the bone. By then the gentle susurrus had turned into the drumming of fat raindrops on the windowpane. The children had gone over to the neighbor's to play Black Peter. They left in their wake a tidal wave of disorder, the most familiar objects suddenly novel as they lay in disarray all over the house. A slight draft was descending from the attic room, bringing an unidentifiable smell compounded of flowers and medicine. For no reason at all she entered Mária's room, leaving the door open so she could back out at a moment's notice. The room itself was not large, and the shortage of furniture and the tidiness made it even more cell-like. She was surprised to find the picture of the girl in the wheatfield pinned on the wall. She sat down on the narrow sofa experiencing a chaos of embarrassment and revulsion, although both feelings were saturated by her relentless love for her sister.

A philodendron shoot was rooting in a glass of water and a ladybug sat on one of the pale green but still very luminous leaves. In between the insect's hemispherical hard outer wings, where the closure was not quite complete, the brown tip of a membraneous flight wing protruded like the point of a knife. This seven-spotted little machine was a carnivore (so she had been taught at school). Her fingertip touched the edge of the glass and she shuddered, for her dress was still wet from the rain. The only disruption in the razor-sharp order in the room was the door of a wardrobe that was left open a crack—and she had the childish notion that this was the origin of the draft. She opened the wardrobe, something she had never done before, and began to explore the shelves and the compartment that had hangers, delving into the most ordinary objects. She could feel her heart thumping in her throat. Altogether there were only five dresses hanging there and she was familiar with every one of them, in fact she herself had sewn the green one. Even as they hung there the dresses seemed so alive that she hardly dared to touch them, although the tissue papers serving as protection against dust should have been enough to dispel any illusion of the dresses being alive. There they were: sweaters, lingerie, handkerchiefs, towels, bedlinen, everything neatly folded to the same size, just as in a filing cabinet. Snuggled in their midst were lavender sachets, a few colorful diminutive vials, bars of scented soap in their wrappers and three muslin scarves in wooden rings. A small silver desktop picture frame preserved under glass a photo overexposed in every detail: a landscape and a few people was all that could be made out. Involuntarily her hand crept forth to feel the silks and woollens. At once she was overcome by acute shame, as that pilot had been. She made a quick turn and ran down the wooden stairs. Once downstairs, she was seized by such a wave of numbness that she was unable to account for the several minutes that elapsed. Dazed, she sat down in the glassed-in porch and stared at the steaming garden outside. As if a page had been turned in the family album, Aunt Iduska emerged from behind the hazelnut bushes, carrying her purple-black rustic umbrella, and going through the dahlias she shook the heavy, rain-soaked flowerheads one after another. All the while, the drone of the everoperating radio was filtering from the small back room. The Loire had overflown its banks at Noirt. (Over the years Anita, too, had become proficient in the German and French hydrological vocabularies.)

She could almost hear the sound of time crumbling into a Sahara-like dust.

9

Summer came and went, but the wisp of smoke refused to budge, nor did it fade, like those stains on the oversize dowry bedsheets which prove impervious to bleach.

Traditionally the former Lipovszky tavern would be opened up for the wine harvest season and for the one-day autumn cattle fair. The Lipovszky family died out decades before, and since then no one had ventured to rent the establishment, yet the building showed no signs of aging. Far beyond even the Pándzsó district, it stood solitary by the former charcoal burners' road. Its heavy fieldstone walls enclosed a single oversize taproom with narrow loophole-like windows giving directly on the woods of Dark Hollow. All year long the building resembled some abandoned fortress that not one tourist deemed worthy of visiting (and thereby providing some dialogue for the desolate edifice—no matter how one-sided such colloquies tend to be). In the fall the municipality hired a bartender, waiters and a pig-sticker who slaughtered a few young pigs for the cold kitchen. The carters, whose wagons were loaded up with barrels full of sweet wines, all stopped in here, Amundsen-like explorers of some fertile polar region now sojourning in the security of a long-established base camp. The neighboring Shepherds' Meadow, where each autumn the animals were driven for market, already conjured up the atmosphere of the fair: harvest wagons with their chained wheels slowly dragged about by wily old horses left to their own devices, grazing leisurely while waiting for their masters. The lazily lurching wagons and their continuous creaking cast a nomadic spell on the scene under a veil of moonlight. The tavern's courtyard was soundlessly engulfed and fertilized by rank vegetation. There seemed to be not a trace of recent human intervention, but this impression was superficial. The backyard was separated from the front yard and its lilacs by a hefty woodpile (at least twenty years old, now held together mostly by creeping vines), in back of which discarded soda crates were decaying along with all the refuse thrown there when the tavern was open. From there a narrow footpath led to a hidden little hollow with an ancient elder tree in the middle. Around the tree bits of crushed blue glass were laid out in spiraling circles, like a screw-thread flattened into two dimensions, trailing of stinging nettles behind the palisade fence of the bowling alley. During the harvest weeks bowling balls rumbled by here. First came the whirring approach, then the crash of the pins as they flew about, followed by the ball, careening full tilt up the concave curve of the wood palisade as its momentum rolled it into the groove, to return at a slower pace. The approach.

Gergely, if he pressed his whole body against the palisade, could feel the approach of the ball on his own skin. He was the one who had, earlier in the summer, laid out the spirals around the tree, for no reason at all. He simply needed a secret because he was in love with Mária and he hated his father.

"Father could have been a dead war hero, and everyone would now remember him with reverence," He daydreamed as gently as he used his pocketknife to slice off the wings of junebugs he made to pull matchbox carts. He had elaborated a whole fantasy to go along with all this (using his own vague imaginings liberally sprinkled with bits borrowed from readings)—so that the hatred for his father became transmuted into an uplifting destiny.

The scene of this deeply felt dream was a dense forest (a *dark* forest indeed) where countless paths led toward the clearing, and he was seeing all this from up above, from a gallery formed by the thick boughs. Of course there would be moonlight. All was still, and he could feel the emptiness permeating the thick jungle. It was all like the inside of a green crystal ball. (In this fantasy the moonlight did not prevent him from clearly telling each color apart.) After a while a dull creaking signaled the arrival of ungainly narrow wagons equipped with oversize wheels. The wagons were the length of a human body and were pulled by some invisible force as they headed for the clearing. In the wagons lay all the tired soldiers, naked and blue, with silver medals around their necks, each one marked with a name and a date. The soldiers were exactly alike, except for their bulging eyes. Then all of a sudden hordes of tiny, insect-size musicians materialized (directly plagiarized from a beloved storybook) and in a trice each grew to the size of a boot. They wore red jerkins, buckled shoes, and carried their violins under their arms. There were enough of them for each wagon, and all of them started to play in one single movement, but their playing made no sound so that the melody could only be guessed from the tempo of their bows. Now the soldiers' eyes slowly came to life and began to glow more and more, until, like shells from a gun barrel, they shot from their sockets, each leaving behind a trail of light. And it was as if they took care that everything should happen exactly this way.

This is where Gergely escaped every week. The clerk suspected his son had some secret, but his most persistent interrogations proved unsuccessful. One night, on hearing a noise, the clerk went out to the living room and stood there for several minutes straining his ears; each passing moment he imagined a barely perceptible creak was just melting into the silence on the wooden stairs to the attic.

A few minutes later Anita appeared in the doorway.

Her face could not be seen in the dim light, only the pastel outlines of her nightgown were visible. (There was something astral about her, maybe a piece of a comet's vaporous tail.) The clerk, in his awkward underwear, was leaning against the walnut table, and, although he was better lit up by the moonlight, his hairy legs with their varicose veins were still barely distinguishable from the bent wood table legs. At one and the same time the two of them were like one of those couples married for too many years who wander sleeplessly in an apartment familiar to the point of boredom—and also like a couple of guests at a boarding house who had just met for the first time that evening at dinner, and who know fully well, without needing any words, what woke them in the middle of the night. (The members of the household are sound asleep, the crumbs from the evening meal still litter the tablecloth, the carpet is soft and unfamiliar, the grandfather clock is ticking with an old-fashioned *sordino*.)

"That kid has got to be lying," said the clerk, flopping down into one of the armchairs, as if this were the most natural topic, given the time and the place.

Slowly Anita moved closer. Her voice registered no surprise; she was not fully there.

"What are you talking about?"

"He tells me that an old picture is missing from the Lipovszky tavern..."

(There was a story behind this. Chief Prosecutor Martinkó, upon assuming management of the tavern on behalf of the municipality, had brought over from his own wine press-house a turn-of-the century photogravure as wall decoration. The print depicted two monocled hunters in plus-fours firing shotguns simultaneously at the same rabbit, and hitting instead the backside of an unsuspecting peasant girl—it was most likely a Tyrolean or Bavarian genre picture. The wench, grabbing her rump and her crotch, is jumping high in the air behind a bush, gritting her teeth in a humorous manner; the rabbit is lying low under another bush, while the two monocled hunters exchange "upper crust" glances. Martinkó, who was a frequent guest at the taproom during the harvest weeks, never let an occasion slip by for passing off one of his *bons mots* about the picture. His wit found a far greater captive audience here than back in his own press-house.)

"And the picture is not missing?" asked Anita.

"Yes it is. Six weeks ago Martinkó had it taken down for re-framing, because it got mildewed. But how on earth did the kid know about this? Granted, if someone looked through one of the windows, the picture could be seen. But what is he doing loitering that far from home? And anyway, what business does he have there? He's full of secrets at home, and he's full of secrets away from home."

"Oh, he could have heard someone talking about it."

"That's exactly what he claims! But I know he's lying."

"Because we are able to tell what is true and what is not!" And Miss Farda's dog came to her mind. And what were her animals saying farewell to, with such irrevocable tameness? "It is all so unclear...," she mumbled, and broke into convulsive sobs.

The clerk stared at her tear-soaked face in sensual bewilderment, at the same time experiencing a rush of greedy desire for this body still redolent with the smell of the bed, a body he knew in every intimate detail. He pulled her into his lap, and they looked at each other, face to face. They had always known, yet were still surprised every time, that at times like this the pupil of the eye leads such an independent existence, like some creature trapped in amber, unable to break out. Meanwhile the silk ripped with a soft swersh as he grabbed the décolletage of the nightgown and pulled it lower and lower to press his palm against the moist handful of hair. They slid down to the carpet without breaking eye contact. All this time Gergely sat squatting at the head of the attic stairs, as in a gallery.

10

Ábel Porszki, contrary to the clerk's expectations, did not live to be eighty-eight but died that autumn at the age of seventy-nine. Only one distant relative arrived for his funeral, a matronly old lady from beyond the Tisza River, in the eastern part of the country. The reporter from the county paper tried to interview her about the old court case and Porszki's acquittal, but the lady was unwilling to answer any of his questions. On the other hand, out of the blue she volunteered certain information that turned out to be of a sensational nature. She said that all those fables retailed back in the old days in the county paper by Syrasius Acrotophorius were pure hogwash. Similarly, the details of that notorious cow-ride serenade had been completely misconstrued. Quite simply, this was what happened. The murdered mayor's father had gotten Porszki's mother with child, at a time when she was still unmarried. Since he already had a wife he refused responsibility for the child and insisted on an abortion. The mother was unwilling to go along with this and found herself a husband instead. Later, when both parties became widowed, the elder Böröcz wanted to resume the old liaison and blackmailed the woman, threatening to reveal the secret of her child's paternity. The future land registrar, who was an adolescent at the time, was unaware of the reasons behind the conflict, but on one occasion, hearing his mother's appeal for help, he pulled a knife on the man who was creating a disturbance in their house. The midnight serenade was in revenge for this incident; riding the cow under their window could also have been simply a crude country squire's jest. In any case, if Porszki was in fact the killer, then he had murdered his own half-brother who had by that time become mayor; and, as an adolescent, he came close to killing the man who—although he did not know this—was in reality his father. MYTHIC DRAMA WITH POSTHUMOUS WITNESS, ran the headline to the lengthy story.

Chief Prosecutor Martinkó, who, at the time of the trial had assisted in evaluating the results of the investigation, maintained in front of friends that old man Porszki had a very good reason for stopping of all places in front of the Martinkó villa in the course of his daily walks. The court had acquitted him only for lack of formal evidence. "Gentlemen, that bench he picked for himself was a *slip of the tongue* belonging to a missing confession."

This succesful new *bon mot* outlasted memories of the Porszki affair itself.

11

Not many people noticed the fresh bouquet of flowers placed each week on the old gentleman's grave. But in any case it would have been difficult to ferret out the identity of the person to whom this act of remembrance meant so much. It was always after dark when Miss Farda set out for the cemetery, and she took care to conceal the flowers in a linen bag.

And anyway, the Chief Prosecutor possessed only one bit of personal information about the reclusive spinster: whenever it rained she obsessively kept playing the same Chopin étude. The bouquet remained a mystery of minor importance.

12

October was the month of remembrance, devoted to the martyrs who died for freedom. The idea of freedom penetrated through even the most banal opening. Even the fishermen who brought their catch to town in carts covered with reed mats now weighed out their fish with a self-conscious solemnity. The gates of the Casino and the Club were bedecked with flowers, and the national flag was displayed with a black ribbon. The town grew noticeably quieter. Manners became more refined, a more gentle style prevailed. Death was now seen as something beautiful and dignified, giving rise to daydreams of all sorts that were never brought out in the open; people merely dropped hints that they had other things in mind than what others thought of them. What landscape did one see through that final window? How important could it be, on death row, to scrape away an annoying flake of skin from one's hand, to wipe away that crust of rheum from the eye, to smooth a crease on the bed? Old sayings came to be recalled: *the unhappy soul condemned to execution—in his despair he turned to the priest as he would to a policeman, lost in a strange town.* The word "homeland" became like grandmother's lacy underthings for children who want to liven up their home theater with an intimate, authentic prop. It was possible to lose one's way in the midst of historical sorrows that followed one after another, thus perpetuating grief. Only true believers and independent-minded humanists acknowledged that it was always a matter of some human being dying, even if it was the "dog-headed Tartar"; that the executioner, too, had to end up where the "dog-headed" one started out: that all was evened out in the legitimacy of the headstone's brightly polished parentheses.

In the face of a stubborn coincidence that reigned for many years, it did not rain on this martyrs' day.

With unchanging modesty the sinuous wisp of smoke continued to hang on in the background.

"So what about Haynau?* The same thing happened to him. He

* (Translator's note: Haynau was the Austrian general commonly held most responsible for the cruel reprisals after the 1848/49 revolution, including the execution of former cabinet ministers and generals at Arad in October 1849.)

kept returning to the scene. Blood is hard to scrape off. He planned on growing old here; this is where he bought land. Were you gentlemen aware that he secretly established a charity for wounded revolutionary veterans?"

The trees in the Casino park were centuries old. Expenses be damned, the municipality had purchased the turreted wooden hunting lodge from the Millennial Exposition of 1896 and ever since then it has served well into autumn each year as a beer and card hall. The feeble October sun shone through the window. It had grown tired since the Millennium. The cards were given a rest. Smoke curled in the air and the wicker chairs creaked.

"Ah well."

"Yes, Haynau."

"He couldn't find farmhands to work his land."

"Not at first."

"That's how it is."

"They say he turned into a confirmed Melancholicus in his old age."

"Is it any wonder? It's unlikely that his mind was filled with the kind of thoughts old Aunt Trézsi had; remember her? That poor old woman, every time she did the wash she imagined the basin was the manger and the laundry was the stable."

"You know they stoned him in London when they found out who he was."

"And what are we Hungarians supposed to do? Wait patiently?"

"*Ame nesciri...*" nodded the parish priest Máté Csanaki (who was Mária's confessor).

A little later a dull crash signaled that one of the bored waiters flattened the whole set of bowling pins with a single ball. A furze thicket lined the sides of the bowling alley; sunshine glazed the top of the hedge a finely spun honey, while down below the solid mass of the thicket congealed into grainy green-black caviar.

The clerk, too, happened to drop in at the Casino on this day, but sat, out of self-imposed modesty, some distance away from the table occupied by the habitués. He let his gaze stray for a long time in the direction of the parish priest. He would have liked to have a talk with the priest, but would have been at a loss to explain about what.

That night he lied to Anita: he said he had been at the Club.

"It is rather strange, wouldn't you say, that the parish priest never stops in there..."

They were sitting under the lamp with the red shade. Anita stared contemplatively at "The Farewell of the Animals"; the red-hot stylus in her hand was slowly cooling down. This time of the year, when the storm windows were put back on the porch, the warmth of the glowing charcoal felt good.

"*Ame nesciri...* That's a pretty good quote for October," murmured the clerk, and looked up. "What do you suppose Mária is doing? Is she going to keep on loving her dead, without ever getting to know herself?"

They looked at each other for a long time, with a searching gaze. Outside the dead leaves rustled, restlessly seeking a place for the night. Mirrored in the windowpane, through some prodigy of reflection, a diminutive duplicate of their lamp shone in the depths of the garden, as in a tunnel that is always ready to be of service.

13

Mária was not one who would forget about the October anniversary. She lit black candles in the evening instead of turning on the light. She had a stressful day at the laundry: dysentery had ravaged one of the wards (with two fatalities) and the chef had already been placed under arrest. At home she took another bath and lay down naked on the rag carpet, her arms spread out, her thighs pressed together, and closed her eyes. Her day was done.

14

December arrived, and the first day with the smell of snow hanging in the air.

Anita found an open book on the Biedermeier card table by the staircase. "... I am the question mark between two worlds, I am the cripple tied to the arch of the bridge spanning the abyss..."

Some old-fashioned confessional author, the name did not mean anything to her. She had not even known that they had this book on their shelves.

Lately these early morning hours never failed to produce a tightness in her throat. The children were off at school, or at the neighbor's. They left behind an unholy mess; their trail proliferated all through the house.

The night before she dreamed that she had finished her picture. The lynx did make a furtive attempt to leap over the stream and upset the tranquility of the scene, but was unable to do so in the end.

15

The archive was warm and smelled of coal gas and dust; the Silesian cast-iron stove, barricaded behind asbestos screens, glowed a cozy red.

Looking out at the marketplace the clerk was able to see the first snow. It lay upon everything like a blanket of shrived guano.

For some time now he no longer thought of Porszki with the old repulsion—he was now caught up in the "affair" as a fly on sticky paper.

Soon it would be eight years that at Christmastime—when she always became so talkative and cheerful—Mária had let out a trivial detail of her childhood. "I had such a high forehead," she reminisced, "and yet the way mother combed my hair was to push it a bit down in the front. She really knew how to mother me."

Even a trifle of this sort was enough to create a storm of laughter for no particular reason, it had been that kind of a boisterously jolly time.

Only Anita added a comment "just to keep the record straight", wiping the tears of laughter from her eyes, remarking that they both had the same mother.

This was what the clerk mused about in between dossiers.

That night there had been no mention of the surreptitious silence that weighed on the relationship between Anita and her father. It had been her father's wish that she should inherit the emerald ring after his death, and his will specified that he wanted Anita, and not her mother, to wash his body before he was laid out.

16

Aunt Iduska, as she had promised, returned from the Hangos Ranch on Christmas morning laden with gifts of all kinds. Among them there was a rock-hard old fungus that had a three-fold curvature, as if a snake had frozen in a pose for the photographer, and had never been told that the picture had long ago been taken, so that the poor creature became its own funerary monument. There was also a fossilized snail, and a trouser button from 1848, "which had been sewn on by the poor count himself, to set an example for the gentry!" Her lace-up boots were left unshined this morning, the white stains drying into map-like contours. "That's how slushy it was over there!" she reported.

There were a few other preliminary gifts to be handed out at breakfast. This was a day of great family meals.

The breakfast table was laid on the heated porch.

This cozy nook, glassed in on three sides, provided a shelter that jutted out of the house, penetrating into the snow-laden garden with a snug taunt: You outside world, you may be freezing, but we are warm and toasty inside!

Ágota had her own way of appreciating the privileges of the porch. She pawed in the direction of the snow-burdened branch that grazed the window, and crowed, exultant, "You're not getting any of our warm, you're not!"

A real Christmastime mood prevailed.

The old gentleman showed up at the table, wearing a beret, starched collar and starched cuffs—this was at lunchtime! And immediately a storm of laughter greeted him, because, although he had his collar on all right, his necktie was missing! "What are you saying! I am saving that for dinner!" he announced sternly, and was mollified only when Mária, in her endearing way, inquired if there was any further news from Noirt. For these occasions Mária always wore black, but she also pinned in her black hair a small tea rose of such a passionate shade of crimson that it rendered any other color instantly noncompetitive.

In the afternoon, while Anita and the clerk were trimming the tree, Mária took the children for a walk. With an innate sense of tact the children acknowledged and grew accustomed to seeing a

totally different Mária come to life on this day. But the change did
not occur from one moment to the next, it unfolded gradually:
already in the morning they could hear her softly singing in the
bathroom, "Fairest rose of all! Fairest rose of all!..." — which
could have been taken as a boast had her humility not been
common knowledge.

It was at lunchtime that her laughter bubbled up for the first
time. Gergely put salt on his poppyseed cake. She teased him,
"It's all the same for Master Gergely, everything turns sweet in
Master Gergely's mouth!" Gergely blushed crimson and hid his
hands under the overhanging edge of the tablecloth.

Little Andris was the only one who periodically forgot to take
part in the general merriment. He had one particularly delicate
way of turning his head that called to mind the sideways turn of a
deer's antlered head—as if a universe more deeply initiated than
ours were turning on its axis then. His glance came to rest on a
bare branch unadorned by snow because it was crowded in under
the eaves of the woodshed. That poor branch.

Mária took the children for a walk as far as Ritka Street, where
the Pándzsó began. A wind was blowing but it went around them.
Everywhere the road was alive with powdery whirlpools, so many
small twisters raising funnels of snow and pouring these into other
funnels that arose from nowhere. Or else a long corridor would
open up, through which they all walked as on a plank laid down
over turbulent waters. "All of this is physics," she was explaining
to Gergely, "as we move forward, our bodies are displacing
volumes of snow in front of us, as if we were shoveling it." She
wanted to see if the boy went for the easy bait; after all, he was
already taking physics at school. But he did not bite. Instead, he
lagged behind a small ways, mass-producing snowballs and
throwing them with a shout of "Now!", so that they whizzed past
Mária on her left or her right, and she was supposed to raise a
hand in time to indicate the side on which the snowball would
arrive. For a long time she kept making incorrect guesses, then all
at once she went on a wizard streak, getting it right every time, as
if she were able to see the boy taking aim in a snow-crystal mirror
in front of her. But then, on making an abrupt turn, she instantly
received a direct hit smack in the middle of her high forehead. It

was a classic head shot—and she, a fountain of sparkles. She burst out laughing. And as the melting snow slid down to her mouth she stuck out her tongue to lap it up eagerly. The children found her mesmerizing and danced around her, even little Andris, except that instead of prancing, he picked up a handful of snow to lick it with total absorption, as if to verify that there were no tricks in this extraordinary game.

They turned back as the blue twilight began to descend.

The clerk and Anita spent an almost wordless afternoon in the house full of the scent of evergreens, as if they were apprehensive about being found out and caught, afraid of pronouncing some forbidden word before its time. Through the fancy grillwork in the tile stove's door lanky tentacles of firelight kept escaping in a soundless dance, and in their light bits of tinsel glittered on the carpet, along with the silvery white glimmer of imitation snow. And the pair of them, like a well-matched old butler and chambermaid, dressed the tree with meticulous care, as if it were a right honorable lord or lady. The scene possessed a beauty that was, above all, an uneasy one.

Even when she stood on a chair Anita had to stretch in order to reach the star at the top of the tree. This operation took several minutes because the clamp was loose and the star kept tilting. As she strove upward on her tiptoes the longitudinal muscles of her calf bulged one after another. Again, the clerk was unable to say what was on his mind, something like, Geezes, what is so antique about these quick undulations under the skin? It was as if some frivolous creature were sliding around under a tight-fitting wrap.

"Now Ágota would say that you are a short angel," he chuckled softly, and passed a palm over her calf.

"Because I can't reach as high as the star?"

She jumped down from the chair and began to pick the tinsel filaments from her hair.

"Leave the gray hairs in."

"Yes, we'll water them and let them grow." Slowly she moved over to a window, spread her arms and leaned against the windowframe. She resembled a T-shaped solid suddenly coming forth into view. "What have you been up to?"

"I bought some eight-year old vintage. From that special place, up on Hermit Hill…"

"You sure know how to pick'em!" Anita laughed heartily.

"And you?"

"Last night I finished the picture."

"Could that be what we are afraid of?"

After a moment's silence they proceeded to the bathroom to shower and dress in time for the lighting of the candles. Anita rubbed both of them with a scented oily lotion from an opalescent bottle. They luxuriated in the scent as the bubbling foam was washed away and splashed back on by the shower spray. It was like shedding one's skin over and over again.

"Listen to this: little Andris came home yesterday and said that today the priests are going to eat little Jesus three times…"

"Ah the cannibalistic golden age!" The bubbles made the clerk sneeze.

Anita slapped him. "You dummy!"

17

The old man also possessed a grass-green beret, its edges curling up like some toy rain gutter, and he wore this with his green tie at the dinner table. Aunt Iduska showed up wearing a matronly long skirt with a silken-glowing brown blouse to match, and the everpresent knitted scarf over her arm. The clerk sported a blue blazer that called to mind some graduation ball for overage highschool students. Anita wore an ash-blue polka-dot dress with blinding white piqué, sort of like a servant girl's holiday best. Mária had on the same outfit as in the morning, but she replaced the rose in her hair with a fresh one. For a lark, the children wore each other's clothes all mixed up, insofar as size differences permitted. Little Andris, since there was no way he could fit into one of Ágota's skirts, tied one in front and one in back on his belt. Ágota decked herself out in Andris's red cotton sweater that reached down to her knees; to go with it she chose her favorite yellow socks and black pumps. Gergely had to make do with Ágota's straw hat which he plopped on the crown of his head at a rakish angle "like a cowboy" and strapped to his chin with a rubber band. Everyone agreed that the gala and the masquerade had been a roaring success. And the mayfly magic of the sparklers made everyone believe that things like this existed in secret, even when they were not in evidence.

"The Farewell of the Animals" occupied the place of honor upon a card table, surrounded by heaps of presents. The demijohn was spouting its vintage wine through the open mouth of an alabaster Bacchus head set in a cork ring. They were already past the stuffed turkey, and the children were having their "bird's milk" (floating islands of frothy meringue in yellow vanilla-milk), when Mária asked for a moment's silence for the girl found dead in the wheatfield. A somewhat uncertain silence ensued; they went along with her request, but no one felt the need to go into the affair in detail all over again. Ágota was quietly slurping the sweet sauce, Andris kept slipping his finger through a brown-rimmed cigarette burnhole in the table cloth, and Gergely had an irrepressible urge to urinate but did not dare to leave the table. The resurgent wind slashed grains of ice against the windows.

Mária's eyelashes cast long downward shadows as she stared at her hands clasped in her lap. Anita was leaning on her elbow with a similar immobility and was watching her husband; her relaxed fingers curled the way a cat's paw dangles forgotten in mid-air while the feline attention is focused on something. As the clerk ceremonially refilled their glasses the demijohn emitted an occasional loud glug. The silence was indeed deep. Aunt Iduska's eyes roved over the family with an outsider's sentiment, although this glance melted away almost untraceably in that pale blue and still bright pair of eyes. Grandfather's tongue was moving around his dentures, the mark of one who ruminates out of habit. He was the first to raise his glass.

"Well then...!"

From here on the conviviality spread in a wildfire of quite unforeseeable improvisations.

"Mária, won't you tell us your most beautiful story!" suggested the clerk, thereby abruptly quickening something, no one knew what. The children were lying on their bellies near the pile of presents, or were running around, always managing to stop at someone's chair and grasp the chair's arm for a breather, only to race off again, in a sudden fit of indifference to adults, and hurry back to the tree. Barely perceptible air currents hovered in the room as a result of these constant comings and goings, so that grandfather's pipe smoke was not able to waft undisturbed like King Mirab's everchanging island in South Sea waters.

Mária's far-off glance paused on Gergely before taking in the rest of the gathering.

"Once upon a time we found baby chickens in the bedsheets at the laundry. I'm serious! There was a huge pile left to be done in the afternoon, there was no time to send it up to be ironed, so we left the pile lying in a corner, not very neat, that's true, but it was all squeaky clean. Oh, you know... like when a whole tribe of Arabs throw down their burnooses, there would be time to do them the next morning... You know what I mean! That's how we left things. A huge pile of bedlinen! All full of nooks and crannies, folds, tunnels, openings, hollows and chasms, like the snowy Carpathian mountains, and it is nighttime, there are no bears or wolves, only the bleached white silence, but even this can only be guessed by the smell, because in the dark even the whites are pitch-black—and then, out of the blue, those baby chickens! They started to come out of all those nooks and crannies like yellow pearls rolling off a string! And there was no hen anywhere! How they got there, God only knows. But does it really matter? Someone must know."

The spellbound children were waiting for the rest of the story.

Aunt Iduska kept nodding her head, her amazement somewhat tempered by envy.

"Upon my soul... Did that really happen?"

The clerk emptied his glass.

"Mária is determined to win."

"Oh, what are you saying," Anita gently reproved.

"Why, who could tell a more beautiful story? Let's hear it!"

"What do you mean, more beautiful... I don't get it...." muttered grandfather.

"There was a secret hole and that's where they got in," Gergely laughed awkwardly.

"And, and? Let's hear some guesses," said the clerk, filling the glasses again.

"They came through... the heating pipes!"

"Through the chimney!"

The wave of laughter swept Ágota back under the Christmas tree. Andris sat on the rocking horse and laid his head on its black mane.

"Wait... Where are you going?" asked the clerk, surprised.

"I'll bring the coffee," Anita said, and went out with her arms folded.

Mária made a move as if to follow, then remained seated.

Her eyes met the clerk's eyes the way the point of one stick hesitantly touches the point of another one in midair.

There was a short pause.

For lack of anything better to do, Gergely lit up a sparkler.

The last sparks were flickering away when Anita reappeared with the porcelain coffee pot: it was time for the ritual of distributing the sugar cubes dipped in coffee.

After this, the board game known as Clever Turtle was spread out on the table.

Based on the fall of the dice, the race ran from cradle to extreme old age. The first goal was to grasp a trickily suspended baby rattle, and as long as one was unsuccessful—that is, as long as one kept rolling wastefully high numbers—one had to crawl back to the cradle. Or else—as long as you were unable to flawlessly recite in one breath the following tongue twister: "*Az ipafai papnak fapipája van, az ipafai papi pipa papi fapipa*"—it was back to the nursery for you. In a similar vein, the ambitious young fop eventually gets stood up, the penny-pinching millionaire goes broke, the world-conquering general is demoted to barracks orderly without a single stripe, the loudmouth cabinet minister ends up as announcer at a railway station and the devil takes the hypochondriac.

Andris and grandfather were neck and neck almost a whole lap ahead of the pack. The others were mostly just treading water instead of advancing, forever falling back into what they were aiming to leave behind. This was indeed a sly game, one that turned out to award victory to old age and death, while the losers remained forever young in the arena, going over the same things to the point of boredom. Everyone was totally absorbed in the competition, vying to be the first to receive that rubber-tipped cane so they could shuffle off toward that splendid wheelchair surrounded by grandchildren.

In the meantime the wind continued unabated, although it changed tactics: instead of ramming with explosive bursts against the cracks in the window-frames, it commenced to lean against the wall with a steady roar, in a leisurely, unhurried fashion. The end result, after all, was certain. The lamp's green shade hung only a few inches over everyone's heads, and this intimacy descending on them all the more clearly demarcated that circle within which—here, and not anywhere else—one had to find happiness.

Mária rolled a six.

"So you see, she doesn't really want to win!" laughed Anita.

Mária blushed.

The vintage wine began to show its effects on the clerk. He sat down next to Mária and at the next turn the two of them—each cupping a hand against the other's—shook and rolled the dice in tandem.

Ágota conked out around ten. She dropped off from one moment to the next, laying her head on the tablecloth. She woke with a start to the sound of the glass chimes of the striking clock, and everyone tittered and applauded the event.

"Some competitor you are!"

But it was obvious that the communal part of the evening was nearing its end.

"We'll continue tomorrow, children! Christmas lasts more than one day. The world isn't going to fall apart if we go to sleep now—especially since no one won the game yet—do you hear me, Gergely? You should be the one to set a good example!"

"Here is to Queen Justitia!" The clerk raised his glass high.

Aunt Iduska was rolling with laughter. She was under the impression that Justitia was some kind of funny new-fangled name.

"We too are coming soon," Mária consoled the children.

The room gradually grew quiet. The five of them remained in the lamp's green glow. Their faces registered a wilting freshness, as befits an occasion that is still open-ended, with nothing resolved as yet. Only the old man's face indicated that he would not have minded retiring with the children.

He broke the silence. "Did I tell you? A catastrophe is in the making in the Mosel Valley. There hasn't been this much snow in twenty years. There is going to be sadness in Trier. The bells are going to be tolling in Coblenz, and Trier will be in mourning."

They all looked at him with some indulgence, as at an idiot savant.

Anita prepared a fresh batch of coffee; the clerk kept on drinking more wine. Mária was plinking the piano keys with one finger.

The evening went by without any comment about "The Farewell of the Animals" other than the one or two initial exclamations of "Oh how beautiful! How lovely!" at the time when the still life of presents was unveiled for viewing. True, the picture had been in the works long enough, for months on end everyone had had a chance to witness those anxiety-ridden stoppages and sudden resumptions of work. And so by now they got used to the new inhabitants of the house, whose farewell would from now on be timely every day, always *now*.

18

For the time being the children still shared the same rather crowded and fabulously messy bedroom. Ágota had her couch in one corner; the two boys shared a military bunk bed, the lower half belonging to Andris and Gergely perched in the upper berth. (Only after grandfather and Aunt Iduska were gone would each child have his or her own bedroom.)

On the wall between the couch and the bunk bed hung a pious picture: a guardian angel leading two little children across a narrow plank bridging a ravine. The plank was barely wide enough to allow passage for two children side by side, yet the guardian angel, instead of watching them from behind, insisted on marching right between the children, thus forcing them within a hair's breadth of the plank's edge.

Gergely, although he would have had trouble explaining the word, held a *cynical* opinion of the depiction.

19

The small town snuggled stock-still under the snow.

The Pirnitzer department store's frosted glass sign hung crooked above the sidewalk. Its support had broken, twisted cable ends pointed into the air, and the frozen snow capping it all somehow finalized the picture.

Bright moonlight illuminated the ever-shifting powdery snow.

There were no recognizable tracks on the sidewalk or in the street except for the parallel imprints of a sleigh cutting across the town from the Pándzsó to the train station. Someone on an urgent late-night mission.

In the blue-black sky the wisp of smoke received an oblique sidelight: it had steadfastly kept its form, as if it had become increasingly preoccupied by permanence.

20

The expression on the old gentleman's face seemed to say, "One more pipeful and it's bedtime."

They switched the radio's tuner from the Budapest station, and via some mysterious fadeout the ethereally sexless sound of the Boys' Choir sang out from Vienna, bringing with it a totally different kind of familiar intimacy. It stayed on in the background as one possible variant of audible silence.

"At times like this, Aunt Iduska, all you can see at your Hangos Ranch is the tip of a chimney and nothing else. *'The snow has blown over the road...'* Whooosh..." The clerk lowered his voice.

"Oh, you're all such children," protested Aunt Iduska, overcome by emotion, and swept breadcrumbs toward herself with the edge of her palm.

"And we don't have bears any more. Those days are gone."

"Yes, all gone." Iduska sighed. "And yet when General Perczel was recruiting soldiers for the revolution, there were still plenty of bears roaming around."

"Ah, freedom's red blossom!"

"My, how you wax poetic," commented Anita.

The clerk unexpectedly kissed his wife on the mouth, pressing against her the way a red rubber patch is pressed on a puncture hole of an inner tube until it bonds. But he was unable to force his cigarette-pickled tongue in between her clenched teeth.

"Yuk, you slimy thing!" Anita shoved him away, laughing.

The old gentleman looked on, puffing his pipe, the way one looks on at the coupling of smaller animals such as cats or dogs.

"No, I was wrong before. Trier will be ringing the bells, and Coblenz will have the worse flood. The same thing happened six years ago when everyone predicted it the other way around."

Sulking theatrically, the clerk changed his seat to be next to Mária. The sisters' faces became set in identical smiles that lasted for some frozen moments, as if they had intended to check on each other by means of this mirroring.

"It turned out pretty well this year... a four-day holiday!

A chance to get something done, right?" And he leaned his chin on Mária's shoulder. "Aren't all the bedsheets off on vacation?"

"You are not in the least bit drunk," said Mária, still with the same smile.

"Of course not. The sleigh is running... If there are no bears, we'll take a doe ...two does!"

"All the way through Arcadia?"

"Yes... Why not. Although, if I remember correctly, Artemis did not care where, as long as there was game in the bush..."

"Was there any snow in Arcadia?"

"Of course! Winter, summer, the snow is always the same there... snow blossoms!"

"And what does grandfather say?"

"Please leave me out of this. You should ask the children. You're getting very rambunctious."

"Another glass?"

"Oh, for a nightcap, all right. It'll put me to sleep."

"And you, Anita?"

"Up the high mountain, I never walk unscared, laaa-la-la... laa-la." She unbuttoned her blouse down to the waist and, spinning around slowly, sat down again. "Yes, please. We are totally blotto."

"How about you, Mária?"

"Just some seltzer, please."

"Just some seltzer. There you go."

"I'll tell you, if anyone cares to hear." The old getleman leaned on an elbow. "Flood control, embankments... It's all baloney. A flood is never more destructive than when it breaks through a dike. Then all those fine old customs become useless: drums, alarms, warning fires, too late—here comes the flood! When all that planned floodcontrol was brought in, the old timers would tell you, some years the whole region was burying the drowned. Before that, you see, in the old days you could calculate it to the inch, the terrain did its job, all those hills and deep valleys, and hollows, they all served as obstacles, so that the white-cap high water advanced nice and easy, there was always something in the way to hold it down..."

"Yes there was," the clerk said to himself, and as he jerked his hand his glass tipped over. He spread a thick layer of salt on the red spill. "A bit of pre-wash," he murmured.

"Honey, that will never come out."

They had a fairly good idea of what was in store—the old gentleman had recourse to a comprehensive wealth of expertise in the ways of the waters, whenever "the devil got into them". He would bring up life-saving catchment basins, slippery embankments, boggy declivities, bifurcating drainage troughs, anything that served to tame raging waters. Plus all types of arenas, shoals, mounds of earthworks, crescent-shaped heights of levees!

"There was that Balázs-Bottom Pond down by Bogra, it would swallow up high water like it had a hole in the bottom. This town never saw a flood until the embankments were built for the water to break through."

"Grandfather is a conservative revolutionary!"

Aunt Iduska's clear blue eyes lit up in agreement.

"That's how it was at the Hangos Ranch too, they even escaped the farm land reapportioning that way. Just imagine, when the surveyor showed up they misdirected his cart so that he couldn't even find the land he came to measure..." She laughed with dry delight. "But this is supposed to be a secret!"

Gradually they grew silent, as if they had politely struggled from anecdote to anecdote to the background music of the *Sängerknaben*—although not entirely without prospects.

Unnoticed, Anita slipped into a reverie, staring at her artwork.

"They say we are a true clan... Do you feel that way, too?"

"What do you mean?"

"Well, what do you think! Our poor father..." her glance slid past Mária's. "And then mother..."

"In Arcadia everyone stays together. We learned that in school."

Aunt Iduska had never known the long-deceased parents, but whenever they were mentioned she broke into fervent tears. In one swoop spirits flagged; even though all night long no one had made even a passing reference to Mária's fiancé. But his person had always been a tacit taboo in the family; they had never even seen his photo or known his name, although that was still no reason for the tactful silence. On the contrary, the exact opposite could have been expected, just as the clerk was in no way put off by the prevailing fog of mystery whenever he spun his fantasies about Porszki. And yet it never occurred to him to imagine what Mária's fiancé had been like. Somehow any endeavor of the kind was discouraged by the young woman's open enigma. Perhaps like an eccentric Schlemiel, who possesses a shadow, a shadow that is always there but can never be seen? They sat in silence around the abandoned game board that still lay on the table. Anita was tossing around one of the dice, then she flicked it over to Mária, who passed it onto the clerk. That was where the circuit closed—the old gentleman was nodding out, and Iduska was too busy sobbing. They knew precisely how loudly they could talk without being overheard by the two older people; it was like having a conversation near a sleeping child. Anita wanted the clerk to speak. "Speak: we are all ears!" she said, but the clerk merely looked from one sister to the other, and hiccuped nastily. Mária made no effort to hide her disdain for such lapses in good taste, that this sort of thing made her shudder slightly; that this was not something she understood, this kind of talk was too explicit for her. But at the same time she made an effort to smile. "Why are you insisting on cheating at any cost ... There is nothing wrong with you. Throw the dice, do it all in the open!" Anita sipped her wine and, letting her eyes rest on Mária's high forehead, blew absentminded bubbles in her drink, like a small child who is left unattended. The clerk obediently picked up and dropped one of the dice. But is was not a real throw; the dice got caught in an ironing crease in the tablecloth and did not lie flat on its side. "And so nobody wins!" He chuckled, and hiccuped again. Mária's response was that she, too, started to blow bubbles in the seltzer in her glass and giggled in conspiracy with Anita. For a moment the clerk was confused by their mockery, but his uncertainty seemed to make him even more patronizing in the next instant. "That's right... The two of you make a beautiful pair of twins... Even if you are nothing of the sort!" And using a gentle force he took hold of their wrists and pressed their palms together so that Anita and Mária were compelled to interlink fingers in the manner of a betrothed couple. Then he proceeded to graze his lips against one fingertip after another while intoning the well-known nursery rhyme, "This little piggie is Anita's... this little piggie is Mária's..." "All done, no more," continued Anita with the same intonation. Aunt Iduska, suppressing a yawn, cautiously pulled the colorful game board out of the way, taking care that the players' pieces all stayed in place for the next day's conclusion of the game. Anita waited for this small adjustment to be made, then she freed her hand and stood up so that her light-blue camisole bulged like a solid ball in her unbuttoned blouse. She stepped over to the radio. The others thought that she was trying to find another station, but instead she waved conspiratorially to Mária, "Come here for a second!" Putting her arms tightly around her sister, she whispered something in her ear. Smiling in embarassment, Mária tried to free herself, but Anita did not let her. On top of the radio, left over from the afternoon's tree decoration was a box imprinted with pine trees, containing the coarsely ground sticky paper snow that was used for delicately dusting the branches of the Christmas tree. Anita now grabbed a fistful and whitened her own face and her sister's. Then they turned to face the table. The childish prank was so effective that all three of them were silenced for a moment: the two expressionless larval faces were almost ritualistic, like the windswept rocks smeared with white clay on the island of Ortygia.

The clerk's smile broadened into a gawky grin.

"Little lambs..." he mumbled.

But now Mária said that this was enough. Abruptly coming to her senses she brought her hand to her face as if to pull away the besmirched skin, but only managed to claw stripes into her mask. "Excuse me, I'm going up," she said, and before they could say anything, she hurried off toward the attic stairs. The clerk started out after her, but Anita pulled him back. "Wait... You're staying here! This is too much..." "You wait for me here. Go and sit with the old folks," said the clerk. With unflappable calm he unwrapped Anita's hands from himself and gave her face a perfunctory caress.

Just as Mária did, he took the steps two at a time, but at a much slower and more leisurely pace.

21

It was impossible to tell how much of what happened was perceived by Aunt Iduska. After wiping the fake snow from her face with a handkerchief Anita returned to sit down at the table. Asleep, his head having found a comfortable place on the cushioned back of the chair, the old gentleman fit into this deceptively traditional tableau to provide a touch bordering on kitsch. Silence permeated the room, and later the dull thuds and crashes filtering down from the attic, speeding up and then pausing horrendously for seconds at a time. The attic room sat above the apartment like some sturdily framed wooden box, like a wooden cage in which the long-maned horses of the itinerant circus are transported. It is a winding road, the wagons rattle along on their small wheels; swaying on the wire stretched over the cast-iron cooking stove and the tin washbasin hang costumes, wigs, sequined tutus, body-hugging sheer tights lit up by the rising sun. The landscape rolls by behind the bars of the undersized windows. On narrow mattresses, under colorful rags, blankets and robes sweaty, tired, familial bodies stretch out in abandoned forays into each other's sultry labyrinths and dense body heat. Anita could visualize to the last detail Mária pinned down on the rag carpet, sidelit by snowy moonlight. She could see the assertively hard, virginal breasts as her sister offers herself, as in triumphant revenge she first penetrates herself to the hilt, then raises her wet finger in a feeble gesture of self-defense. And again came a confusion of thuds and crashes, a hobbled trotting in one place. Aunt Iduska imagined it was the wind pushing the snow from the steep roof down onto the rosebeds—and she smiled at the thought, consoled by the idea that the roses would now have a thicker blanket of snow.

Toward eleven Anita suggested that they all retire to their beds, (it would be a pardonable sin if they did not set out for midnight mass in such a blizzard). With a sweeping gesture she embraced and kissed Iduska, leaving no room for her even to think of protesting. "See, we are left as the last of the Mohicans..." Then she woke her father-in-law and walked both of them to their rooms.

When she returned to the dining room the clerk was already seated at the table. He was drenched and unfamiliar, like a horse driven through the night.

22

Around three in the morning they woke with a start. After a moment they sank back into deep dreams. They slept in old-fashioned beds with wooden boards at both ends, and no matter how tightly they wedged the two beds together there always remained a slight gap that was further exaggerated by the separately tucked-in sheets and the forever cold wood edges.

The weather cleared. It was a starry night, the wind had driven away the clouds.

The clerk was not fully awake yet. Only his sensory organs were functioning with a heightened, lethargic sensitiveness. As he reached over to Anita, he felt around until he found her hand on her belly and, in a reciprocated gesture, his fingers interlaced with hers. At first he did not know what felt so unusual, but then realized that the emerald ring she had never worn was on Anita's finger. After palpating it all around he tried to pull it off, twisting ever so gently, but with a movement that was just as gentle Anita curled her fingers and did not let him. For a long time they lay there without moving or saying anything, but their hands remained interlocked. That was how they fell asleep.

In his dream the clerk was approached several times by an enormously enlarged panorama: it was early spring, the Pándzsó was swimming in moonlight, and up on the ridges all of them were on the way to Hangos Ranch, led by Aunt Iduska, followed by the old gentleman, the children, and the three of them bringing up the rear, everyone carrying a bundle as big as would fit on the end of a forked stick. Nor was the unswerving wisp of smoke missing from this dream image: it was anchored in the same spot it had occupied for months. As they passed along the ridge he would have liked to put into words some prayer of forgiveness, to say it out loud so the others could hear it: "Remain Nameless, let there be witness to the beauty of misery," but the highflown sentence could not be voiced. When he awoke, Anita was already on the porch setting the table for the festive breakfast.

PÉTER ESTERHÁZY

THE TRANSPORTERS

Translated by Ferenc Takács

So they have got here at last! So the transporters did get here at last. Their bellows hack the dawn into pieces—the dawn is frayed, tattered, grey and worn—silence is fragile and empty. I have seen the dread faces of my sisters!—wild and fierce! wild and fierce!— For God's sake, my darlings, what has happened?

Through the thin apertures of the jalousies, the frothy bridles of hard-driven horses—the youthful drivers up in the seats, yes, it was their bellows, coming from their faces rosy with cold, while they were leaning over, steering their steeds with fastidious coquetry. The reins were flying in the air, thin ice chimed under the iron-tyred wheels. Here! here!—A muddy, murky dawn! The clock started ticking loudly, squeeze the clock between your thighs, my sisters cried, wrap that damned clock up in the folds of your skirt. Our greatest need is silence now.

The transporters, they were resting, sprawled out, in the back of their wagons, like leisurely gentlemen or like the hills. And in their heavy furcoats! Their sight offsets those skinny little, weak little driver lads, with their pathetically thin mousy hair, the chequered cloth of their peaked caps worn, jug-eared, the skin of their hands blue and purple from the cold. Their white bloodless color has a name: paleness. True, their teeth glint as they smile, when they were wriggling their wagons around bends and corners with a maximum of noisy fuss and horseplay, but how would that compare to those wolfskin coats? Who is it who has to keep moving his limbs and move he must? The transporters themselves—like some heavy objects, —lean, with their treetrunk bodies, against the soft corn-silk lining of the wagons, the air is yellow with the steam of their breath around their lips, as if they have been smoking cigars. Their faces wide, they are bearded almost without exception, though not unfriendly, no, not at all!—lying in their respective forage racks, they laugh, across the distance, short and quiet laughs to one another. They understand one another, I can see that much. Their thighs are of heroic proportions, their trousers cannot help being tight.

Our faithful dogs are in a rage, baring their teeth, tugging at their eternal chains, but they put no fright into anyone: the lads did not annoy them and no irrevocable order came from the transporters. Very likely, they reclined among their furs, sulking.

Your faces, my elder sisters, opened up in a blush, but why are your faces blooming with wrath?—Why would you drag me away, prying me off the windowpane?—my nails are trying to get some purchase—green and sharp little flakes of paint—you little frog, why were they hissing this? you little frog, get the devil out of here! why did the rattle the jalousies made when the tug-of-war burst them open, startle them into jumping back from the window? What a light. Do you understand now why your hearts go into secret palpitations when you see me approaching? A clear sound crossed the silence, a light spot of color spread across the crystal, light filled the eye that... An incredible rainbow, an almost improbable freshness was caressing my eyes. The light is driving a wedge into me, the luminous horses, the steam, the sound, the noise, the frozen mud, and the forbidding barns around. Darlings, why do you flatten yourselves against the wall? Be happy, no need for this pride, for this anguish.

This was the moment when a majestic figure, a full-bodied transporter got up on his knee, and at a mere motion of his hand his driver, as if in a fit, stops the vehicle, he is yellow, like his traces, the master is now standing with legs apart, his man answers him with a proud wink of the eye, and upwards, upwards, he is pointing up to our room—a bright stare took me in and its radiance broke the seashell in which my heart lay slumbering. The horses were whinnying, pawing the ground, the courtyard awhirl with icy dust. Dawn: diverse traces; who knows. Bodies are shivering, the whining of my sisters fills me with lunatic strength, a feeling without defiance, fear and limitations possesses me suddenly, it is jubilation—there are random traces of exhalation on the windowpane, a thin nightshirt held tight in front of my belly, crease and squeeze, yes, he is looking at me, his furcoat swings and rocks around his body like a churchbell.

Voilà votre mort, monsieur!*, I cried enthusiastically. On the porch there is mother—mummy who is shouting at the hounds as she shouts at her unruly brats, us. In the room, it is dark again, piercingly, madly dark—you miserable, miserable fool, my sisters plaintively cried, they got back into their beds, pretended sleep. I begged them and begged them to let me get in between the two of you, but to no avail, poor sleepy girls, the sleep, it was pretended; I wanted to embrace, but there was no way. I wanted to embrace, but there was no way. I hated you, with the same heart I still have and hated the space that surrounds, hated our room...

Our room! Oh how many awakenings on the soft and warm bellies of my sisters! My belly is different: if I feel it, I feel muscle and bone, muscle, bone. My sisters are beautiful, those who I love are beautiful, I watch them furtively, enraptured, their pirouetting in front of our mirrors, preening themselves sourly—face-powder flying and descending like dust on the weeds by the road—and then a finger, when on its own, draws conduits on the pane, difficult scrawls. Sometimes they let me zip their clothes up and I was afraid that I might pinch the alabaster skin of their backs. When evening came their faces were colorless, themselves taciturn, sitting on the edge of their beds, their hands quiet in their laps. And I went down on my knees in front of them, untied ribbons, untied their faces, untied their stares, I lay my head in their tired laps and, while there, caressed their backs with a circling movement of my hand, and sneaked more and more upwards, stretching myself; then I got up to the bed, panting, squatted next to them on the bed, rubbing the goose-flesh of their arms—my sisters!—the top of their hands smelled of onions and perfumes, and finally I stroked their hair, which by that time of the day shed all its curliness—mane and hair—their hair that went straight back on their scalps, flatly and with some suspicious glitter, held tight in a practical knot by a thin red, yellow or black rubberband, otherwise used on jamjars; I untied this as well and took their whisps among my fondling fingers. Like puppets, motionless, they suffered it all. I unclad them, their gluey clothes sticking to their bodies—I pre-warmed their beds with my own body and they embraced each other and closed their eyes.

* That's how you are going to die, mister.

The day was happily over, I kept saying in my heart, oh little Zsófi, little Zsófi, they whisper and go to sleep as if they were dead. But when morning came their bellies were warm and downy and my cheek was again getting warm on their navels when I woke up. Their belly-grumble was silvery music to my ears.

Woe betide you, dogs! Iron waistcoats caving in, horses dying the death of a horse driven to death. By the time spring is here again, there will be grass and meadow-saffron growing on your graves, also, dog's-tooth violets. *(textual corruption),* what is this noise now? Stag-beatle-thunder, I answered. In the doorway, there is light again, mummy stands, untying the sheaves of light, her beautiful plump body radiating rosily, loving is good because loving is hard, I rushed up to her, embraced her wildly, I pushed my head between her bosoms—exaggeration all, herself included, that cherry-red lipstick, thick greasy makeup, insistent scents and lotions, by just looking at her I feel rich, I feel that no harm can ever be done to me. Her fingers are yellow with nicotine, her arms are freckled, the skin on the heels of her feet is hard like rocks. I am fat as the moon is silvery, she says.

Oh my little one, she breathed and tears trickled over her broad face, oh my makeup will be a soggy mess, she sniffed angrily right away, get into your Sunday best, put on your pearly necklace and, above all, take a pair of clean fresh knickers, you little bitch! Oh good: this is a felicitous answer.

How we admire the bluntness of mother, the straightness and drive with which she gets across the obscure drift of her speech, how much I understand her in these moments! Wash yourself, she said, and the rest will take care of itself, and with this my education was finished as far as she was concerned. For some time we went down to the village regularly—to see the countess, that's what mother called her, the countess, and, true enough, she was a woman with some experience, widely traveled and intelligent, she has seen life and a few places, like Pozsony, Szabadka, even Pest—I feel pity for those who are frightened by as little as a century or for those whose love would not extend beyond the borders of a country, she did have the splendid knack of adding her comments to the contingencies of the day in an altogether natural manner;—comments which were now addressed to us personally, especially to me, for my edification, for my education.

Let me see you, she said on the first occasion, she clasped my face in her cool hard palms, you've got a nice facey, a nice little facey-wacey. Those unforgettable excursions! The crusty bread, the squeaking hamper: noises, tablecloth on the grass, white, green—green—The sky, the sea: a layer of thick living, where life swarms and passes away... I feel wonder at the wonderful shape of the seagull, at the line it flies in. How was this flying ship made? My tall sisters were basking radiantly in the sun, twirling their silky parasols, we are going to pick mushrooms, they said with a giggle, I had to squint, I felt dizzy because of so much heavy light, we are going to pick mushrooms, the long murderous wandering among the quivering shadows of August—and frequently we shed our frilly clothes to take a dip in the brook and while we were thus sporting ourselves, changing ourselves at our momentary will, from wild little rascals into gentle little creatures—the countess, in a dress of summer, summer, high neck and black color, went on guarding, as it were, us and the creased smile around her lips showed that she knew full well what her momentary role was: and she may well find this role painful and disheartening. The countess! On the bank of the brook, a helmet made of wolfram, ladled full with honey and tar. In a while my sisters grew petulant and started talking about *ennui* in beautiful and heart-rending words—that there is nothing more difficult to bear than total inaction, without passion or the everyday grind or fun and effort. In moments like this, one feels all the more keenly one's nothingness, abandonment, insufficiency, *dependence,* helplessness and emptiness. From the depths of one's soul there wells up a feeling of boredom, melancholy, dejection, sadness, sorrow, vexation and despair. You've got a nice little facey-wacey—I had no fear of anybody—I did not know what fear was—nothing is more precious than what you are in others and what others are in yourself—Above, all things are one! Above, all things are one! They gave me a course in walking, too, my sisters unrolled a blood-red silk ribbon in the garden and I had to walk on the ribbon as if it had been the thin crest of a dike besieged by perfidious waves of water from both sides while they were shouting words of adoration, all of them, even the countess included, great, little Zsófi, congratulations, just look at her, look at her sweet little buttocks, how sweetly the little bitch is wriggling it!

This extatic turmoil got wilder and wilder, we whirled and danced, then flushed—dance and dance—and if I landed in the big soft arms of mummy, as a kind of conciliatory gesture, since I had been fawning on the countess in an altogether slavish manner, mummy embraced me, touched to her heart, my little love, how nimble your flesh is, she said.

But then I placed my hand on her waist, look, on her swirling full waist, I placed my hand on her back, on her queenly wide back, I placed my hand on her belly, on her soft round belly, I placed my hand between her breasts, between her immense marbly breasts—oh no—oh no, mummy, you are mistaken and it surprizes me that you are mistaken, your flesh is luminous and radiant, I envy you because all I feel in myself is muscle only, muscle everywhere, as if I were a piece of underdone meat— muscle and bone—limits, limits everywhere, limits, your are immense and I love you—come on, my little darling, you said this beautifully, just as a young one should, immaturely, my belly is fatty, you can see that, my waist is blunt in shape, my breasts are sagging satchels, my back is full of folds of bacon and my buttocks would not bear mentioning.

Mummy!

I put on my crispy white Sunday dress, though it was not Sunday, no, Sunday it was not, and I put on the white cool pair of knickers. Oh the silence! My sisters no longer pretended sleep, they were getting dressed—how much chatter and giggling, panting, gasping and wrestling on other occasions of the same nature. They told me off when I started preening myself in front of the mirror, just to be funny—just wait, they hissed threateningly—but why are you so glum today, dears? Are not the ones who just arrived those we have always anticipated in words of color and dreams of hue? Are not... My sisters came at me furiously and tore at me—your sanctimony makes us sick. Just wait. It is early, for me, to take for wisdom what is only melancholy, indifference, disillusionment... My sisters knealing on my thin arm—curses, curses.

There is only one mother. Mummy is dressed in her scarlet frock with silvery trimming, the wide Chinese girdle, the silk slippers, the wonderful rainbowy plumes in her ebony-black hair, dazzlement, a constant wind, the tiny glass pendants of the Viennese chandelier clink against each other tinkling—wind, breeze, breath.

Aren't you afraid, little Zsófi? Oh mother, if I dared to answer you now with all the rudeness of my sincerity, yes, I dare, and I would say, no, I do not understand what you are trying to ask, how can one be afraid of what is, is not what is not much more fearful, (what is, is not; what is not, is), hush, hush, be quiet you stupid naughty girl, be quiet. A feeling of gentle tickling on our lips, wavering and tinkling, rainbow-plumes, laughter and fireworks again. Ah, tais-toi, je ne veux plus!*, my sister cries, mother is kissing me. A rude sound suddenly, where from, it is hard to say promptly, from outside, from inside, from beyond the door or what, it is a thin mocking laughter, though the voice is deep—well, fine, if there is no fear, fine and very well, the little miss would not even think of, why should the calf be afraid on the way to the abattoir—there is no fear—though it was the little miss who said that what is not is much more fearful—The cowardly sigh of relief, so it is you, Dummy, it is you, frightening people as if we have not had enough trouble already, hold the reins of your sharp tongue or I'd wring your neck if you had one, you little runt!

Who is this mummy? A miserable creature—you could see him in the wagon, he was squatting at the feet of your transporter, true, he hardly stuck out of his sack—a kitten on its way to the river—He does not believe in anything. He says the stars are so many barren rocks, the lamp is not a lamp, table is no table, children are no children.—Unruly offspring. Marjonka, dear, I see you would let me perish as is your wont, said the creature whom our dear mother has just called Dummy, and he stepped out of the embrace of the shadows—he was the Knight.

A scream then, quickly, how ugly he is, my stomach convulsed with retching, hand pressed tight over gasping mouth—it is late—Yes, the Knight nodded in assent, yes, Princess—he was a

* Oh shut up, that's enough of that!

tiny little man, in a blue sailor's blouse, with soiled gym-shoes on his feet—fluttering, fluffy shoestrings, worn greyish-blue pair of linen trousers—his head is stuck on his trunk, like some white puff-ball—some ungainly hump on his right knee, as if he were hunch-kneed.

My visible horror brings silence. It is obvious, the sad Knight said and made his leg flutter a little, like a clown whose leg is devoid of—bones. It is obvious, Princess, that a stubborn injury has been giving me trouble.

I am sorry, I said as politeness required and my sincerity prompted—why feel sorry? why feel pain?—on the Knight's brow, skin creased up in a double arch, dragging his eyebrows with it, his face of parchment, his tired face, thin face, his face—He was laughing—his bad teeth, blunted—My Princess, you are sorry for me? for this homeless scum of the earth, this helpless pig in the poke to whom the Lord granted a more than necessary amount of reason and a less than sufficient amount of talent or power, my little girl! after all it is not me who is bleached, hot and decorated with bunting—a cheap necklace on a dark and hard morning, bleached, hot and decorated with bunting—It is obvious; and my stately master, blessed be his name for a while, is sitting in the sooty kitchen there, dipping bread into what is left of his bacon and eggs—You!—consider who you are squandering your earthly suffering on, do not squander it on an unworthy lout like me, save it, it is valuable!, save it for yourself, you will see crying is not just *utile* but *dulce* as well. Dulce...

What it means to be vermin? he said, darkly, to himself... The miserable creature is harebrained, weak in the head, halfwitted, a shriek from mother — Oh, said the Knight, flower, dawn—Now why don't you shut your trap, quoth our dear mother, and then the little girl, myself: dear stranger, I do not understand your words and even if I understood what I cannot even conceive of, there is no reason why, but I saw you and I see you, I saw you, now I know, at the bottom of a forage rack, curled up at the huge boot of a transporter, and I see you now, worn and yearning in your flesh and all this makes me bitter and full of accusations...

Troth, little girl, your tender age makes you brash and bold, a mere child, that is what you are, whence is your courage to advise others—Whence is your courage to observe?—irritated crumble, little man. I may have blushed, though I did smile, I knew I could not be mistaken—there was something in me that wanted to be told, I could not help it so there was nothing praiseworthy in telling it, and the Knight fell silent, no, my dear, you are bitter and full of accusations, so you are wrong, fail to notice the goodness of man, the light of the world, the radiance we all exude—Mangy dogs, we bleed on pillows, we are beautiful. Then, later, only clumsy and immortal.—I do not. I do not want to blame you, I want to be your support instead, with all the strength of my youth, do not ask me why, strength is always in excess, it is weakness that is always just about sufficient, the former is exuberance, bubbling over, turbulence...

So this is all, this is it, this much only which is due to me, this, this intention is my only present? this overflow, bubbles running down the side of a copper cauldron, this impersonal much, what would be left for anybody?!—Do not speak like this, my good man, do not think me proud as I believe there will be times when you will need me, the Knight said stamping angrily—and I went on, now less certain, accept me, sir, for a friend, and, look, accept my little hand as a pledge to our friendship. Suddenly, the Knight grew solemn, he was sour and uppish, and at this point I must confess I was frightened because I never thought I could be that important, teach me, the man said, what is true purity: it is not that bloodlessness that sets you apart from things, it is the drive that penetrates all beauty. Declare now what true love is: not the futile dread of sins but the bold purpose with which every man, in concert with all others, tries to pry open the gates of life... and he offered his hand for the taking and so did I, shyly, afraid to touching his, but just as my finger was about to touch his, he snatched his hand away—You silly little goose, he shouted with tears in his eyes. Will you stop this nonsense, mummy said simply —dear stupid Knight, stupid bright Knight.

What the hell, Marjonka, what is this pandemonium?!—the transporter!—his face was in the dark, in the mysterious play of light and dark, the strong and smelly paraffin lamps of the kitchen, like two spotlights, put an aura around him with such a light—as if struck by a thunderbolt—his silhouette started to radiate, light, light, light, light and power came off in all directions from his outline, wavering, flaming, oh yes, the transporter is indeed a handsome man—His huge thighs set a-straddle—His thick oaktree of a trunk — His horseneck of a neck and his red and stately—The strong-muscled head, yes, I see him, I see him, it is him—and me! me! me!—I am his pair and companion, I am his, dazzled by what I saw there and thought there, mother disappeared from sight, she who covered us with her warm body, the poor Knight faded, dragging away his sickly stunted body, I was dazzled by this new light—Knight!—this was what we spoke about, the light of the world, I exist only, I am the one who is, and the transporter, and this is light.

Foot stumbles in its devotion, rigid and stiff, and the little girl is dragging herself up, from the cold stone, the applebasket over-turned, winter apples caroming, rolling in all directions, they are so many globes, there will be a brownish spot where they were. Is this frog the one? My belly feels cold—the puniest most rigid object might explode with an all-shattering energy or might suddenly acquire a quality of miraculous hyperactivity if the complement it needs and expects is granted it. I will have to detach myself from emotions with resolution!!! the best there is, believe me, the best there is, first class, only you be careful, fresh, you know, fresh as today's strawberries.—What strawberries, thou blabbering old hag—you'll get a kick up the backside, what are you on about strawberries for in the dead of winter? Or are they some hothouse specialities, thou lustful witch? Mulier amicta sole! Thou, woman clad in sunlight, draw nearer, sit down here quickly—the laughter of mother floating in the air, I like to hear it: as if a flock of birds took off for their journey or just threw themselves up in the air unpredictably, tell her, Marjonka, tell her to stay here in the kitchen, stay where she is, sitting. Stay there where you are sitting, mulier amicta sole!

There came and went this new, sweet and heavy morning. Lord, have mercy upon me, Lord, have mercy upon me. I pressed my cold back to the ledge of the fireplace, there was a brisk shower of sparks over the cooking-stove, large pots were tossed this way and that. The kitchen filled up with people, with silvery smoke—the sideshow of drivers, then the Knight with downturned eyes, the transporters sat around the rough wooden table, sampling our foul wine from our pewter goblets, if only you could excuse us, my good sirs, my sisters, pretty and fresh, offered their excuses, but last year's vintage was a complete waste, the Sun refused to extend His tender mercies over our vineyard, all sweat and industry was to no avail and we had plenty of trouble with rust.

It was sheer luck, dear sisters, the Knight said softly, that you were able to resort to certain manuals of viticulture which my good masters, in the infinity of their goodness, at the beginning of time—oh yes, it was luck, indeed, the tranporters nodded laughing, indeed it was. Strong men, their shirts giving off a compound odour of bacon and sweat, they are beautiful, the Knight, seeing my enthusiastic blush, nodded, you are right, girl, they are beautiful because they are sufficient to themselves, they are their own measure, they are beautiful as all existing facts are beautiful —all there is! This is not quite possible since things can be beautiful only if things can be ugly as well. The ugly is what is missing, the Knight stated. He enjoyed being close to me, he half-leaned to me with his rickety little body, he drew his knees up caressing them unwittingly. Yes. The hour is running away among myriads of roses, in the intoxicated rapture of crimson wines, running noisily into the dream of night, mother and my sisters in the hard laps of the transporters, their big palms shoveling them up—the hour is pleasant, mother is trying to block the transporter from my sight with her body, nevertheless I know everything, nothing is hidden from me. This is what I believe. And I wait.

Some sound started to seep through the clatter of the kitchen, through the noise of laughter and sizzling fire, some remote and unpleasant sound, sustained howling, then quick and sharp whining—here everybody provided for plentifully, the howling of dogs intensified into a frenzy—these are our sheepdogs—what's that?, mother asked, extricating herself from the embrace, what's that? We, local people, glanced at each other, saw premonition in each other's eyes. The transporters did not move—what's that?, said mother again—a brave, brave woman—Bravery! was that the word? I heard the word: bravery, stop this mumbling, Dummy, the transporter told him casually. An answer in trepidation, brave woman, oh God what is going to happen to us...

Fine, Dummy, we like it when you speak and when you speak in this manner, we like it if you are our living conscience, we like it when you are witty and entertaining and when you do not spare us your scornful and scourging words, courage de luxe!* because, yes, you can afford to be morally pure and it is perhaps not a vain hope that some of your eternity will trickle down to us—we like... er... your defiance—not that we do not know what you keep throwing at us in accusation, we know it, but everything has its own place, you were born for this role, we, for some other—as if our faces were pierced by hundreds of tiny black needles; though we would not be happy if we caught you being ungrateful, after all you are part of us, curled up in your sack, we do the rounds together, firewood, coal, firewood, coal, you join in in our streetcry—and one must fill one's stomach somehow—up with the curtain! whatever you do there is no other alternative, it is either believing or negating or doubting—we must always have a second thought and judge everything by its light while we speak in the dialect of the people—we calmly rush into the abyss even if we manage to block it from our sight somehow—negating, believing and wisely doubting is to man what running is to a horse.

All right then, my little darling, we understand each other and we are not unduly disgusted, and he put his black hairy paw, as a kind brother would, on the shoulder of the Knight—don't! touch! me!—shrieking; the transporter, unconcerned, nodded:—I am bored. Give me my cloak, please. Knight, mentally, bows his head—in our misery the only consolation we have is amusement and still it is our greatest misery. Because it is which chiefly distracts us from being properly concerned with ourselves and is the unnoticed cause of our ruin. Without amusement we would live in boredom, but this boredom would prompt us to find some surer and more meaningful way of alleviating it. But amusement entertains us and leads us to death unnoticed. They have not found remedy for death, for misery, for ignorance. But, as they

* the luxury of courage

still wanted to live happily, they came upon the idea of simply ignoring these.

You just keep shooting off your mouth, you kinky-legged kibitzer, but mark my word, I do not permit anyone to tarnish man and the progress of man—man, even in his lustful desires, is great because he was able to set his desires in order and reshape them through the image of love—Marjonka!—the transporter's cry!

The dogs fell silent. What have you done, you blackguards? What do you mean what? So what? What *have* we done? They did it as if they were in the shadows, young lads, transporters, what was it... what was it...

They showed us some rind of bacon, teasing us, we slipped them something to eat all right, blue, the blue rind of bacon. Murderers! mother howled, foul—come on, come on, the transporters said, fidgeting uneasily, the face of mother is a red spot, her forehead turned inside out, her eyes glazed, she has drunk a lot, too, the men started to leave, uneasily, easy does it, Marjonka—I was also laughing, they heaved up my sprites of sisters and mother, as if they were sheaves of corn, huzzaing and tallyhoing, they were running with them as if they were sacks of flour, doors whammed shut—a block splintered, its pieces flew—everybody was waiting for this, colorful noise, for this, immense pandemonium. So was I. Things happen too fast.

Empty spaces, indeed—o o my little sister, the Knight was mocking me, we were sitting there alone like abandoned children: always. Does it hurt?—I asked him and placed my hand on his arthritic-looking knee. The Knight blushed and some strange heat welled up in me, I felt infinitely small, pliant and as accommodating as a baby—the broken, prematurely old and bitter face of the Knight which still could not help revealing some purity—beauty which shines among us for those who can recognize it—I felt dizzy, my thighs felt dizzy, all my muscles felt dizzy, I was already flying in my imagination: I am the possibility!—but then I started shrinking, it was a bad, sickening, uncertain feeling — it pierced me to the bone and beyond—We reached a limit, ah yes, we reached a limit, I cried and gripped his knee hard, beyond and even further, more inside, deep, deep—I love you.

161

May God grant me the capacity to hear and make others able to feel, with an almost happy rapture, the infinite music of things. It is only love that is able to move all things existing. Silence, light, white, field, bough, wind: that is what we are. And then, suddenly, the fear—fear and trembling. Let us escape!, I cried.

Escape? Escape to where? And, first of all, *who from?* Come on, little Zsófi...

This is unbearable weakness, I started shaking him, do something, you pig. I shrieked—He hushed me, there, there, we are going to escape, we leave it all behind, we'll disappear into the woods, into our woods, there is a rumor that a few lads from the manor have already disappeared there, we will arm ourselves with muskets, sticks, stones and arrows, dig trenches, take plenty of bread and bacon with us and... and the Knight fell silent.— Excuse me. I am a coward.—Who spoke of winning? Holding out is everything.—Very early I was initiated into the doctrine that in terms of infinity victory is victory while in terms of finiteness it is—suffering. That sad guardian of the kirk. Kirk-guard. It is not solving problems that is difficult; it is posing them. — What is truer will out, what is better will happen. This is what I think, Knight, and I feel, with icy horror, that love and hatred are equally at home in my heart. Knight! I love you. I hate you. — Justice is with you, Princess, not with the "tired", the future does not belong to those who enjoy themselves. It belongs to the brave for whom the future is important, who untiringly struggle to become purer, to reach ever higher and higher.

Silent, silent—If somebody had had the King of England, the King of Poland and the Queen of Sweden as friends, would he have believed that there would come a time when he would be unable to find rest and refuge in the world?—Silent—You must realize that justice requires us to follow the just while necessity requires us to follow the most powerful. Right without might is helpless; might without right is tyrannical. Mightless right is always defied because there will always be evil persons; rightless might is always open to condemnation. Therefore justice and power must be joined together, justice must be made powerful or the powerful must be made just. Justice can always be contested while power is easily recognizable and uncontestable. That is why there was no way to give power to justice because power defied this by claiming that it itself was just. As men were unable to make what was just powerful as well, they chose to consider what was powerful just as well.

Which of the two fooled us? Our senses or our education? Man is by his nature credulous and faithless, fearful and bold. The attributes of man are dependence, yearning for independence, need. The condition of man is fickleness, boredom, restlessness. —The eternal silence of these infinite spaces fills me with trepidation... There is only one kind of loneliness...

My dear, I am afraid.

I am afraid.

My sisters seemed to cry—stars are barren rocks—I was running, I flung the first door in the corridor open—beds pushed up to each other, a wide and ravaged field, bodies with strangely contorted limbs—oh my God, what is this?—my face icy cold—what is going on?—wasn't it you who called me? wasn't it your feverish voices that broke in the distance?—get the devil out of here!, my sisters shouted, and mother is pressed against the wall, the linen shirt of the transporter flutters freely at his knees, she gestures, quick, little Zsófi, go away. The transporter is howling, why should she go away!— what is this general movement in the room? what is this rhythm, fit and tremor?—what are these words here?—how do they breathe here?—what? what?—mother, like some object, dropped to the floor when the transporter stepped away and let go of her, a frightened retreat, my sisters' crimson faces buried in pillows, the transporter became entangled in his underpants, fell over swearing brassily—he is dragging me, like some object, down with him—sweeps me off my feet—Dummy! help me!

I press my legs together but to no avail—I melted as a handful of grease splashed flat under the blow of a hammer—the transporter gives me pain, beastly pain — his heavy onion smell oozes into me—as if I were torn open, as if my bowels were torn into shreds, as if my heart were torn of my ribcage, as if my ribs were slashed open—my thighs are slippery warmth — my thin thighs get thinner and thinner, my God, what was this talk about light and radiance, it is only, only black blood. The Knight attacked the transporter madly, the transporter hit out without turning towards him, swept him aside, as bears do attacking dogs, away with you!, okay go on hitting my back, hit on a scheme, hit, hit, shrewd little Dummy. The Knight got on his feet, stood there, my face facing up, we see each other, I can't recall a thing—He is crying, crying and shrieking, I can't! I can't! Do! No! He takes the blueish rind of bacon out of his pocket, starts chewing it, he keeps chewing it like some little animal—it is a mad gallop round and round—Froth on his lips — He fell.

I am curtained from what is going on; again, I heard mother wailing, come on, stop this crying, Marjonka, there's a good girl, the voice of the transporter is pleasantly deep and quiet, it is better this way—kept in the family... there you are... bring some meat! Marjonka, bring some meat, meat!

— —

I will perhaps stand in the centre. Perhaps it is evening. Perhaps it is sunset. One thing is certain, it is late. I am alone. I pulsate. In the darkness out there flames are dancing with threatening flashes; the barn is on fire. Hell working without witnesses. Our hopes the stars loom dead. The windowpanes broken, the glassless frames are swinging to and fro, the wind blows billows of black ashes into the rooms. Still, there is fire in the stove. The kitchen table is overturned, chickenbones scattered all around. There is no dog for the bones. My thighs are stuck to the blanket, I feel cold in my inside, I am an open wound, I smell, I smell of sewers, I am apart, take me, oh Lord, to a loneliness I would never have dared to go to on my own.

All right. I drag myself up, it hurts, I put some water in a pot to warm. I fish the washbasin out from under the bed, it squeaks across the floorboards. With my nails I scrape its enamel... I scour it with sand, I scour it with sand.

A wagon is drawing up, it is them, laughing in a whirl, pushing into the room. I feel faintly sick, what is going to happen to us? They keep interrupting one another, the beasts! They have set fire to the barn! Never you mind, mummy says laughing, it was empty anyway. They are still a little drunk or very tired. Their faces are as dusty as weeds by the road. My darlings, I say softly. They chatter and giggle like machines. I managed to get some salt, mother cries. Did you now, Mistress Shrewd, my dear sisters start fooling, what was the price your ladyship paid in her cunning, the tilly of lust into the bargain? No, no, you ungrateful creatures, all you need to know is the wherefores, the ins and outs and wherefores... I had to teach a little driving lad where he belongs... And did you teach him, madam?! You can see for yourselves...

They think, they do, they think they can get away with everything. Well, they can't. No, not at all!, my sisters said, I grabbed his balls with both of my hands, the lousy transporter went green with pain! he was about to flail out, howling, and I told him this was the latest fad straight from Paris... I tried the same but it did not work because he took to it straight away. He probably had swollen balls anyway, the poor lad! Poor, poor lad. —I think mother and family are going to have a good life. And then, finally, my sisters say: And we did not come! No, we didn't. The yokels, they thought we had, but no, *I did not come,* they think they can get away with everything.

Winter is growing on us. A lonely wolf came down to the village. They turn towards me, it is all right, little Zsófi, we are satisfied with you, we saw you haven't an ounce of fear in your body, and Dummy is good for a start, they are laughing, especially as he is finished now and we do not have to worry about his discomfiting schemes any more.

I loved him, I say. So you loved him, the tall girls cry, you loved him, you say, she loves him, they exchange incredulous glances, she loves the fool and mascot of a transporter... You idiot! Couldn't you see what these people were?! Couldn't you see what they were up to?! Would you mess around with people like that?! You good-for-nothing treacherous slut, they are coming at me threateningly, they draw sharp bodkins, die, Zsófia, die you must, so die all traitors. I am about to commence my last prayer, my sisters are reeling with laughter, reel back to their beds, they are sprawled out on the stained yellow butterfly-patterned blanket, they are rolling about wrestling, panting, their teeth flashing. Oh you! Mummy brought in warm water and a mug of milk. Lay the table. Make the bed. Stoke up the fire. Set the dogs loose for the night.

There is no dog. I am sitting in the washbasin. Scraping off, like the enamel earlier, dried flakes of blood. This is my blood. Douching does not hurt me. We have come through again, my sisters say panting in extasy. Yes, yes, we have come through, my darlings, mummy says, she is stroking my hair with her heavy old hand, we have come through, and we have salt, potatoes and parsley.

We all break into the laughter of heartfelt relief.

The novel contains, whether accurately reproduced or in a distorted form, quotations from the works of *Teilhard de Chardin, Søren Kierkegaard, Blaise Pascal, János Pilinszky, Rainer Maria Rilke* and *Géza Szőcs.*

NOTES ON CONTRIBUTORS

GÉZA OTTLIK (1912—1990), novelist, short story writer, essayist. Born and educated in Budapest, he studied physics and mathematics, though his interests soon shifted to literature. His career as a writer started with a number of short stories he published in literary magazines during the 1930s and collected in *Hamisjátékosok* (Swindlers) in 1941. After the war Ottlik, by nature given to scrupulous rewriting and sparsity of output, continued his prewar book-reviewing and literary essayism, translated plays for Budapest theatres and worked as a drama critic. After the Stalinist takeover in Hungary in 1949, he was barred from publishing his own writings and had to make the best of the usual translating and ghost-writing assignments reserved for "the bourgeois-humanistic element" in literature by the Stalinist authorities of culture in the early 1950s. Nevertheless, he managed to survive this difficult period, and he was even able to retain the (admittedly minor) post of Secretary of the then virtually dormant Hungarian P.E.N. Club from 1945 to 1957.

With the publication of his collection of short stories *Hajnali háztetők* (Rooftops at Dawn) in 1957, followed by the appearance of his novel *Iskola a határon* in 1959, Ottlik made a second literary *debut* the strength of which was eventually to lead to the now near-unanimous recognition of the author as perhaps one of the most important major presences in postwar Hungarian fiction.

This reputation is certainly borne out by *Iskola a határon*, which, with the recent death of the author in 1990. remains Ottlik's only exercise in the longer fictional form. Available in English translation under the title *School at the Frontier,* the novel has been variously interpreted as a microcosmic allegory of the nature and dynamics of totalitarian power, as an acute psychological portrayal of the wartime and postwar fortunes of a particular section of the professional middle-classes in Hungary, or as a more general and very analytic fictional inquiry into the ways the human mind attempts to make some kind of potentially self-liberating sense, through remembering and through imagination, of its own constraining past.

During the decades following the publication of the novel, Ottlik's work was short fiction, ranging from traditional variants of the short story to more experimental fictional techniques. These pieces exhibit their author's *penchant* for irony, intellectual paradox and narrative innovation. The story included in the present collection, published originally as "Hajónapló" in 1987, represents Ottlik in this latter mode: "Logbook" is a Borgesian exercise in transfictionalizing certain obsessive paradoxes of national identity, authorship, writing and language. In this it uses, with much ingenuity and wit, fictionalized versions of the personality of some of his Hungarian literary coevals including that of Iván Mándy, novelist and short-story writer (a contributor to this collection): in "Logbook" Mándy appears as "Vice-Admiral Ivo Maandygaard" (where the Joycean condensation of the name makes some rather apt connection between the Hungarian author and Søren Kierkegaard, the protoexistentialist Danish philospher) while the text of Mándy's novella "Left Behind" (see in this collection) also crops up in Ottlik's story, assuming a supportive role in an intertextual poetics of quotation, allusion and paraphrase.

"Logbook" appeared originally as "Hajónapló" in Géza Ottlik, *A valencia rejtély,* Magvető Könyvkiadó, Budapest, 1989.

Works also include *Minden megvan* (Nothings's Lost), short stories, 1969; *Próza* (Prose), short fiction, essays and reviews, 1980; and *A valencia rejtély* (The Valency Enigma), three stories, 1989.

Works available in English translation include *School at the Frontier,* Harcourt, Brace and World, New York, 1966, and "Nothing's Lost," short story, in *Nothing's Lost: Twenty-five Hungarian Short Stories,* Corvina, Budapest, 1988.

IVÁN MÁNDY (b. 1919), short story writer, novelist and playwright, was born in Budapest. It was, indeed, Budapest, or at least a certain distinct area of the Hungarian capital, that soon captured his imagination: ever since his literary *debut* in the 1940s, made secure by his novel *Franciakulcs* (The Spanner) in 1948, his stories and novels have used the same urban landscape of lower middle-class, inner-city Budapest. This is Mándy's country; a poignantly poetical and infinitely evocative fictional rendering of metropolitan decay with its regular components of cobbled streets, of old, dark and rundown apartment blocks, of withered curbside trees in back alleys; a world of boring little cafés with their one-cup-of-coffee-an-afternoon clientele, of small cinemas where only a few old people linger in the vestibule, of pathetic little squares in empty lots, their benches (and the people who seem to have all the time of the world sitting on those benches) slowly rotting away in the cold shade cast by bare sidewalls of derelict houses.

Dwellers of this landscape. Mándy's people are a function of this environment: their lives seem to share the poignant sadness of their quietly and very undramatically decaying surroundings, indeed, their lives are totally conditioned by the frustration, alienation and existential *Angst* so consistently and effectively inscribed in the material detail of the Mándy landscape. The cumulative result of all this is a uniquely philosophical poetry, underpinned by the miracle of the Mándy sentence, the short, stale, almost cliché-like tag that carries, by its textual and contextual isolation, a wealth of submerged meaning and subliminal suggestion. Indeed, it is Mándy's language, the ineffable textural magic of his fiction that produces, out of his deliberately ordinary and *prima facie* rather unpromising material, a bleakly honest vision of human life as a condition of quiet desperation, of existence as something hopelessly and irredeemably lost to Heideggerian inauthenticity. There is, though, empathy and compassion in Mándy's universe; they are elicited whenever the author comes across the dubious workings of man's only (highly doubtful and in the end useless) remedy for the human condition: his infinite capacity for self-delusion Mándy so incisively records in the futile little daydreams, petty duplicities and pitifully modest self aggrandizing ruses of his characters.

In "Left Behind," Mándy's 1986 novella that is reproduced here, an imaginative, if not fantastic, rupture between the Mándy country and the Mándy people is posited, and then as imaginatively resolved, by the author: here, in the story all human presence is, quite inexplicably, gone, the people have departed and all we have now is the landscape. Alien, artificial, entropic and dead, it is now the man-made world of urban dereliction that comes to life and, in a bold trope of personification, acquires a mind that remembers, suffers and mourns; Mándy, in the ultimate fictional act of collapsing his country and his people into one, makes the world of *things,* that manmade universe of dead (and decaying) artifice that have always been, in a sense, the protagonist of his fiction, sing a threnody for humanity.

"Left Behind" appeared originally as Iván Mándy, *Magukra maradtak,* Magvető Könyvkiadó, Budapest, 1986.

Works also include *Mélyvíz* (Deep Water), play, 1961; *A pálya szélén* (On the Fringe), novel, 1963; *Az ördög konyhája* (The Devil's Kitchen), short stories, 1965; *A locsolókocsi* (The Water Wagon), novel, 1965; *Séta a ház körül* (A Walk around the House), short stories, 1966; *Régi idők mozija* (Those Good Old Movies), short stories, 1967; *Mi van Verával?* (How Is Vera These Days?), short stories, 1970; *Mi az, öreg?* (What Is Up, Old Boy?), novel, 1972; *Zsámboky mozija* (Zsámboky's Cinema), novel, 1975; *Strandok, uszodák* (Baths and Swimming-pools), novel, 1984.

Works available in English translation include "The Kitchen Wall," short story, in *44 Hungarian Short Stories,* Corvina, Budapest, 1979; "Ballgame," short story, in *Nothing's Lost; Twenty-five Hungarian Short Stories,* Corvina, Budapest, 1988, and Iván Mándy, *On the Balcony (Selected Short Stories),* translated by Albert Tezla, Corvina, Budapest, 1988.

MIKLÓS MÉSZÖLY (b. 1921), novelist, short story writer, playwright. He studied law, then worked as a newspaper editor. Shortly after his literary *debut* with the short-story collection *Vadvizek* (Floodwater) in 1948 he was barred from publishing his work by the Stalinist officialdom in control of culture. During the morally and politically dangerous early 1950s he found a congenial refuge in the Budapest Puppet Theatre where he worked as a script editor.

With the publication of his new collection of stories *Sötét jelek* (Dark Signs) in 1957, he reentered the Hungarian literary scene. Still, recognition of his stature as an important writer came slowly and ambiguously. It was only with the appearance of his novel *Az atléta halála* (Death of an Athlete) in 1966 that some idea of the quality and the importance of Mészöly's fiction started to take shape in Hungarian literary criticism, though as late as 1976 his novel *Film* (A Movie) still generated critical response in which sympathetic understanding was mixed with rather large doses of irate incomprehension and calculated hostility. It was, however, in the same decade that the emergence of a whole new generation of young Hungarian writers (including, among a number of others, Péter Esterházy whose work is represented in this collection) with their emphasis on fictional experiment and narrative innovation highlighted the centrality of the achievement of older practitioners of the form such as Mészöly who had been previously seen as more or less harmless eccentrics on the fringe, absurdly at odds with, and therefore hopelessly isolated from the mainstream of Hungarian fiction, or, alternatively, not seen at all. Ever since the 1970s Mészöly's reputation has been steadily growing, and nowadays he is generally recognized as an innovator of major significance in postwar Hungarian fiction.

As an innovator and experimenter, Mészöly's emphasis has always been on writing as an intellectual or philosophical activity *per se.* His novels and short stories are concerned with the paradoxical relationship experience has to its fictional transmutation and the enigmatic results of this transmutation. In this he has some significant affinity with postwar experimental literature elsewhere as his consistently self-reflexive concern with the epistemology and ethics of the literary act has its counterpart in the French *nouveau roman* or in American "Postmodern-

ist" fiction. He also represents certain welcome virtues; in all his work he is a writer of muted poise, sparse elegance and quiet self-discipline, in marked contrast with the general tendency in recent Hungarian experimental fiction of gravitating towards conspicuous excess, verbal and technical exuberance and indulgent "bigness" in general.

"Forgiveness," Mészöly's 1984 novella included in this collection, is very much a case in point. Its material is as unemphatic as possible; indeed, it recalls, quite deliberately, a gray area in earlier Hungarian fiction, the realistic small-town story (set, in this case, in the post-World War I period) with its provincial middle-class characters who grind out the days of their severely limited and frustrated lives. This is the kind of all-too-familiar material (in effect, a stale literary convention in Hungarian fiction) Mészöly defamiliarizes in a number of strange, unexpected and sometimes puzzlingly enigmatic ways. He composes several mysterious motifs, all concerned with some idea of timelessness and permanence (like the puff of engine smoke that never disappears from the sky above the railway station) into a subtext of finality. This is the finality of memory (represented metaphorically in the novella by official records, scars, deaths, cemeteries, photographs and pictures) that freezes time into something unchangeable, unforgettable and, by the same token, unforgivable. Also, an analogy to fiction, to the act of writing is quietly suggested: just as for the characters in the story remembering works against forgiveness, the act of writing for the writer is fraught with the burden of unforgiving, of the unavoidable refusal to extend sympathy to one's literary material that is, after all, life. Mészöly offers a richly ambiguous resolution of this dilemma: he concludes his story at Christmas, with its faint hope that his characters can stop remembering and his writing can achieve at least a kind of tentative forgiveness.

"Forgiveness" appeared originally as Miklós Mészöly, *Megbocsátás*, Szépirodalmi Könyvkiadó, Budapest, 1984.

Works also include *Pontos történetek útközben* (Precise Stories *en route*), short stories, 1970; *Film* (A Movie), novel, 1976; *Magasiskola* (The Falcons), novellas and short stories, 1985; *Merre a csillag jár* (Where Stars Wander), short stories, 1985; *Volt egyszer egy Közép-Európa* (Once There Was a Central Europe), short fiction and essays, 1989; and *A pille magánya* (The Loneliness of the Moth), essays, 1989.

Works available in English translation include "Anno," short story, in *The Hungarian P.E.N. — Le P.E.N. Hongrois,* No 22 (1981), and "The Falcons," novella, in *Nothing's Lost: Twenty-five Hungarian Short Stories,* Corvina, Budapest, 1988.

PÉTER ESTERHÁZY (b. 1950), novelist, short story writer, essayist. He published his first short story in 1974, which was soon followed by a short novel and a collection of short stories, or short experimental "fictions." With the publication of his novel *Termelési-regény* (A Novel of Production) in 1979, a book that elicited general critical acclaim as well as unprecedented public response, Esterházy soon became the symbol, figurehead and, in the public eye, the near-cultic idol of a whole generation of young writers (including Péter Nádas, Péter Hajnóczy, Géza Bereményi and others) who appeared on the Hungarian literary scene during the 1970's. Different as they were, these writers were united in their rejection of some of the traditionally and nationally enshrined commitments of mainstream Hungarian fiction: they discarded the conventions of formal realism and socio-political documentarism, these near-automatic postulates for much earlier writing, and opted for a more innovative and self-conscious interest in textual indirection, self-reflexive involvement with the act of writing, allegorical abstraction, parody and pastiche; also, they introduced a more skeptical or tentative estimate as to the epistemological efficacy of writing in coping with present-day reality or realities.

In many ways, Esterházy's *Termelési-regény* was a triumphantly successful summing-up of all these concerns and impulses. It certainly shows Esterházy in full command of his exceptionally bold and rich innovative gifts: his linguistic exuberance, his wonderful sense of parody and pastiche, his weird talent for combining ready-made myths and pieties of the Hungarian mind into shockingly subversive and very funnily evocative collages, of debunking standard fictional procedures by exhilaratingly carnivalesque dislocations, and suggesting a sense of life which is threateningly serious and gloriously playful at the same time.

With his *Függő*, a short novel published in 1981, the richly and playfully polysemous title of which can be rendered as variously as "hanging," "conditional," "suspended," "provisional," and "relative to," Esterházy embarked on a fictional quest that led him into the writing of a series of books, varying in length between the sparse short-story size and proper novelistic bulk; these he collected under the title *Bevezetés a szépirodalomba* (An Introduction to Literature) in 1986. The result is a kind of "supra-novel" where the originally separate pieces now make up various aspects of, and perspectives on, a potential, though technically speaking unwritten, whole. While the book ranges over, in a mode of dense intertextuality of quotation, reproduction, imitation and pastiche, themes of national history, autobiography, literature, philosophy and intellectual history, its pervading concern is with the ontology of the literary act: the coexistence and, also, the paradoxical interpenetration, within the same work, of inaccessibly personal and autobiographical fact and publicly accessible, conspicuously literary artifice.

"The Transporters," which is now one of the constitutive "aspects" or "perspectives" of *Bevezetés a szépirodalomba,* represent this later Esterházy at his most complex. In the subtitle he calls this short, intensely lyrical, almost prosepoem-like text "a novel", though the length and the narrative scope of the work would hardly equal a (traditional) short story. It is, indeed, a paradoxical retreat from the novel; a retreat into a fusion of archetypal and personal experience, filtered through heavily patterned, ornate and richly modulated poetry, and of more general existential statement, carried here by an intertextual strategy of quotation from Pascal, Teilhard de Chardin and others. It is certainly a fusion of extremes; a condensation and, also, a deeply moving and bitterly funny balance of private and public, of the personal and the metaphysical.

"The Transporters" appeared originally as Péter Esterházy, *Fuvarosok,* Magvető Könyvkiadó, Budapest, 1983. This translation was first published in *The Hungarian P.E.N. — Le P.E.N Hongrois,* No 26 (1985).

Works also include *Fancsikó és Pinta* (Fancsikó and Pinta), novel, 1976; *Pápai vizeken ne kalózkodj!* (Make Sure You Avoid Papal Waters, Pirate!), short fiction, 1977; *A szív segédigéi* (Helping Verbs of the Heart), novel, 1985; (Under the pseudonym Lili Csokonai:) *Tizenhét hattyúk* (Seventeen Swans), novel, 1987; and *Hrabal könyve* (The Book of Hrabal), novel, 1990.

Works available in English translation include "No Title; This Isn't It Either," short story, in *Nothing's Lost: Twenty-five Hungarian Short Stories,* Corvina, Budapest, 1988 and *Helping Verbs of the Heart,* Grove Weidenfeld, New York, 1991.

Ferenc Takács